THE PRIORY OF CARTMEL

by

J. C. DICKINSON

D.Litt., M.A., F.S.A., F.R.Hist.S.

D1345204

CICERONE PRESS
Milnthorpe, Cumbria

ISBN 1 85284 071 4
© J. C. Dickinson 1991

PREFACE

CARTMEL PRIORY church enjoys the enviable distinction of being one of the minute number of medieval English monastic places of worship which suffered no serious damage at the Reformation. Since then it has been lovingly tended by its locals with the result that its structure and many of its fittings have survived with little or no damage. Since the publication of the useful article on the priory in Vol. 2. of the *Victoria County History of Lancashire* in 1908, its history has attracted little scientific attention until quite recently. However, Mr Denis King has employed his unique skill on a scientific restoration of the medieval stained glass of the priory and has, most generously, put at my disposal both his unrivalled knowledge of it and his unique colour transparencies. Dr MacLeod Murray (late of the Geological Survey) has recently published a most illuminating study of the site and stone of the priory which shows us at last, which stone the priory took for the extraordinary complex task of rebuilding the cloister and its attendant buildings on the north side of the church. (*Lake Cartmel, a post-glacial lake and its probable effect on the buildings of Cartmel Priory* in Amateur Geologist xiii pt.2. (1990) pp.43-49). My old friend, Mr Arthur Frearson, A.R.I.B.A. has executed an up-to-date plan of the church and has produced the first adequate plan of the curious little gate-house of the priory. The sound structural reasons which led to the erection of the very distinctive diagonal belfry tower of the priory have recently been detailed to me by Mr J. T. Green of British Railway Engineering Dept. The tester of the noble Harrington tomb has been repaired by Miss A. Hulbert. The régime of a house of Austin canons is printed in J. W. Clark *Observations in use at Barnwell priory*. The closing years of the Lancashire monasteries are given masterly coverage in Dr C. Haigh *The Last Days of the Lancashire Monasteries* (1969) and *Reformation and Resistance in Tudor Lancashire* (1975).

Care has been taken here to give this study the ample photographic coverage which it demands. Almost all those of the interior of the church are the very skilled work of Dr J. N. Bate. The magnificent misericords are the equally excellent work of Dr R. C. Swift, late of Birmingham University. For the exterior photographs of Cartmel and Cartmel Fell and that of the choir stalls I myself am responsible. The photo of the Cartmel Fell crucifix was provided by Kendal Museum. For the air photograph I am indebted to the Air Photography Department of Cambridge University.

The author is greatly obliged to the Kirby Archives Trust for a valuable grant towards the cost of publication of this work.

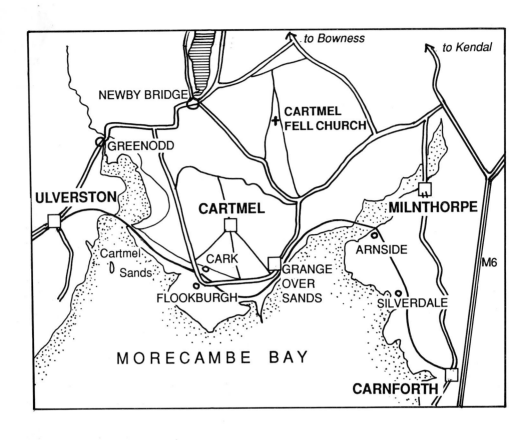

Contents

Cartmel from the air

PART ONE

* * *

HISTORICAL

The Origins

MENTIONS OF CARTMEL before the foundation of the priory are very few indeed and mostly not very helpful, but fortune has left us a sole invaluable reference to it in pre-Conquest times. The *Historia de Sancto Cuthberto* of the so-called "Simeon of Durham", records that Ecgfrith King of Northumbria gave to St. Cuthbert "the land which is called Cartmel and all the Britons in it, and that vill which is called Suthgedluit and whatever pertained to it".[1] The latter place, which Cuthbert put in charge of "the good abbot Cineforth", must be identified with Heversham, which alone in our area is known to have had a monastery in these early times. The fact that Cartmel is a place-name of Scandinavian origin (probably meaning "sand bank by rocky ground") shows us that this entry is not a contemporary one, but does not undermine its veracity. The precise date of the gift is not clear but Ecgfrith ruled Northumbria from 670 to 685 and St. Cuthbert was bishop of Lindisfarne from 685 until his death in 687. It is worthy of note that the donation came just at the time when the Anglian kingdom of Northumbria had pushed its bounds through to the Morecambe Bay area.

It is almost certain that soon after this grant was made, or possibly even earlier, a chapel to provide spiritual sustenance for people of the Cartmel area was set up on Kirkhead, the headland below Allithwaite, which stands out prominently and is easily accessible to those living in neighbouring parts of the coast. Near the chapel, as a document of King John shows us, was a pool called "church pool"[2] of which, as of the chapel itself, no visible remains survive. In the course of the tenth century the area had been engulfed in Viking raids, but whether this chapel survived them we do not know. If it did not, worship would almost certainly have been restored in the area soon after the Conquest. We have no clear evidence on this point though about 1160 we have mention of William "the clerk" of Cartmel.[3] It is virtually certain that a new place of worship had by this time been built, more convenient for the existing inhabitants of the valley, on part of the site later occupied by the priory. The *Domesday Book* of 1086 mentions vills at Birkby and Walton (both very ancient), Newton (an Anglian addition) and also Holker and Kirkby (i.e. "Churchtown"), which latter name was for very long in later times applied to the village now known as Cartmel.[4] Just over a century later the priory came into existence.

It was founded by William Marshall, Earl of Pembroke from 1189 to 1219, whose body and effigy lie in the Temple church in London. Born of a not very important family, by sheer merit he rose to become one of the major figures in national life, being chosen the regent of England after the death of King John (who had a very high regard for him) had led to the accession of the boy King Henry III. His importance is shown by the fact that he was one of the minute number of post-Conquest English barons who inspired a quite lengthy and very interesting biography.[5] His foundation of Cartmel priory quickly followed his marriage to an immensely wealthy heiress, Isabel de Clare, and may have been in part an act of gratitude for this.

The first brethren of the house were acquired from the priory of Bradenstoke in Wiltshire,[6] and belonged to the order of regular canons of St. Augustine, commonly called "the Austin canons".[7] Their life, like that of the Benedictines, had as its dominant concern the maintenance of an elaborate daily round of common worship which began very early in the morning and continued at varying intervals until dark. Its regulations concerning diet and duration of periods of silence were less demanding than those of the Benedictines and Cistercians, from whom they differ also in that, on a very limited scale, their members might undertake parochial work, though there is next to no certain evidence that Cartmel canons did this. Odd as it now seems, our priory was situate in the arch-diocese of York, which then comprised not only the county of Yorkshire, but no small part of Cumbria and a little of Nottinghamshire; Cartmel then pertained to the archdeaconry based at Richmond, far away in the North Riding. It is greatly to be regretted that a series of mishaps has left us only very scanty materials from which to reconstruct the history of Cartmel priory. Its own archives, containing scores of invaluable documents, were evidently sent into storage at York at the time of the Dissolution of the Monasteries, and seem to have been totally destroyed in the civil wars of the seventeenth century, whilst the medieval archives of the arch-deaconry of Richmond, which certainly contained much useful material on Cartmel history, have almost completely disappeared. The records of the archbishops of York, massive though they are, contain very little information concerning Cartmel, as do those of the papacy,

The Church from the south-west (c.1870)

though such information as they do preserve is invaluable, as is a small trickle of references to it in documents of the contemporary English government. As a result of all this there are, in the priory's history multitudinous gaps, large and small, which, for example, make it impossible to reconstruct a complete list of the priors of the house with the precise dates of their periods of office. Happily we have the text of the great foundation charter of the priory.[8] This cannot be precisely dated, but belongs to the period August 1190-96. The process of establishing a monastery in those times was a complex one, and that at Cartmel was probably not completed for some years after this. The first known reference to a prior is to one Daniel, imprecise mention of whom occurs in an undated deed of 1194-8[9] but, a hitherto unnoticed early 16th century note declares that the priory was founded in 1202,[10] perhaps because the foundation stone of the permanent church was laid in that year.

The charter of foundaton is not lengthy, and follows a somewhat unusual pattern. The only territorial endowment which it mentions is "all my land of Cartmel". With it were associated a longish list of rights and privileges, of which the right to mine iron is unusual. It was ordained that the priory was not to be subject in any way to any other monastery. When

11

a new prior was needed canons were to choose two brethren one of whom was to be selected for the office by the founder and his legal successors – a provision which, as we shall see, was shortlived. Information in a papal bull of 1391, which there is no reason to doubt[11] declares that at the time of the foundation of the monastery, it was ordained that the care of the parish altar, which stood formerly where the monastery was situate, should remain in the hands of the prior and convent, and that in the monastic church should be erected, as was afterwards done, an altar of St. Michael, at which the parishioners should be bound to hear mass and receive the sacraments from a priest who was to be appointed and removed by the convent and who might be either a hired secular priest or one of the canons.

The Monastic Site

WHEN A MONASTERY was founded in medieval times, the question of where its complex set of buildings were to be erected was by no means always easy of solution. For it there were three essentials:

1. A fairly considerable area of land which was well drained and at best, convenient as a building site.

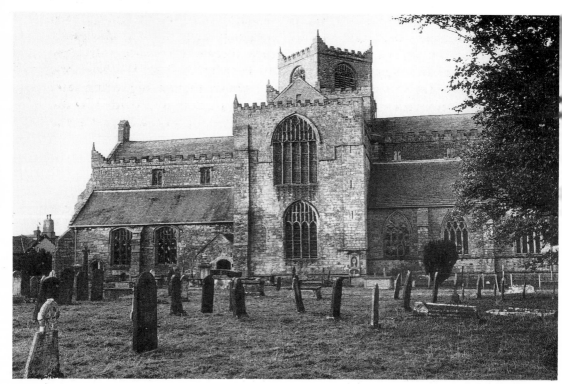

The church from the south. (Photo: W. Unsworth)

12

2. A water supply adequate for five major necessities – drainage, drinking water, washing, fishponds and the watermill (which ground the grain which formed so major a part of the monastic diet).
3. A reasonable amount of local agricultural land and woodland to provide food and fuel.

It was highly desirable that these amenities should be fairly near each other in days when roads and tracks were very poor, and means of travel primitive. Because of the complexity of this problem of siting, the best solution to it was not always at once obvious, and a not insubstantial minority of English monasteries found by experience that it was necessary to abandon their original site in favour of a more convenient one. Although this has not hitherto been suggested, it is at least feasible that such a transference of site took place in Cartmel valley, where good water supplies and fertile land was far from over-abundant. On the eastern side of the area were the massive limestone crags of Hampsfell with very little indeed in the way of either of those. The fells of Newton were similarly unfriendly as well as being hard of access, whilst much of the valley bottom from Cartmel to Cark at that time was undrained land of little or no value. It is within the bounds of possibility, though far from proven, that originally it was intended to build the priory on the flat ground between Hill Mill and the top of Howbarrow. Here was open space linked with a quite considerable water supply which until recently ran a corn mill from a useful sized dam that still remains; the area could also easily have fed fishponds. Woodland and pasture were close at hand, utilised by inhabitants of the very ancient adjacent farm at Walton. We have one piece of evidence to support this theory, which though slight and late, cannot be automatically written off. This is a tradition recorded in the *Lonsdale Magazine* of 1820 which was edited by one who knew the Cartmel area well:

Legend of Cartmel Church

BETTER than six hundred years ago...some monks came over from another country, and finding all this part of the kingdom covered with wood, resolved to build a monastery in some part of the forest. In their rambles they found a hill, which commanded a prospect so beautiful and so extensive, that they were quite charmed with it. They marked out a piece of ground on the summit of the hill, and were preparing to build the church, when a voice spoke to them out of the air, saying "Not there but in a valley, between two rivers, where the one runs north, and the other south." Astonished at this strange command, they marvelled where the valley could be, for they had never seen a valley where two rivers ran in contrary directions. They set out to seek this singular valley, and travelled all through the north of England, but in

13

vain. Wearied with their fruitless search, they were returning to the hill where they had heard the strange voice. On their way back they had to cross the valley, at that time entirely covered with wood. They came at length to a small river, the stream of which ran north. They waded through it, and in about one hundred yards, they found another, the stream of which ran south. They measured the distance between the rivers and placed the church in the middle, upon a little island, of hard ground, in the midst of the morass. The church they dedicated to St. Mary. They also built a small chapel on the hill, where they heard the voice, which they dedicated to St. Bernard. The chapel is long since destroyed but the hill is called Mount Bernard to this day.[12]

The proposed original site – if such it was – had two major disadvantages. Firstly it was a goodish distance away from the old parish church of Cartmel, which already existed on its present site, and whose proximity to the monastic community was clearly desirable for more than one reason. Secondly, it was not central enough to be convenient, being well away from the important coast route across the sands to Lancaster. On the other hand, the site occupied by the existing parish church was very convenient. Close to it ran the River Ay, the only sizeable stream in the area, which at nearby Aynsome proved to have enough power to work a mill, whilst just over Hampsfell, the site later called Grange had, as we shall see, a small but useful harbour. However, as recent research by Dr Murray Mitchell has revealed,[13] the site of the pre-existing parish church was curious and in the long run was to prove unsatisfactory for the monastery. Odd as it seems to us today, the little parish church stood on what was then a smallish and low island in the midst of what was effectively a longish and narrow lake, stretching from Newton to Headless Cross, formed by waters of the River Ay. On this island was an outcrop of the very solid Bannisdale slate, so common in the vicinity, which provided an admirable foundation for the little parish church. The land lying to the south of it had at that time enjoyed much dry weather in recent centuries. Though low-lying it looked sound enough to take the complex array of cloister buildings which the new monastery would need in this position but in the future, as we shall see, this belief was to prove unsound.

Temporal Possessions

THE LOSS OF all the archives of Cartmel priory and of the cartulary which must have existed and would have contained copies or abstracts of most of its legal documents, makes it impossible to get that detailed view of its possessions which we have for Furness Abbey, where the surviving

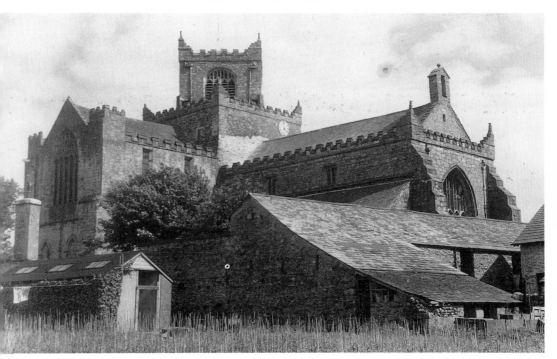

The church from the north-west

cartularies have provided material for six volumes of printed text, which show us, incidentally, that this abbey possessed a small but very useful piece of property in the Cartmel area. This was a grant made in the period 1162-90 by Thomas, son of Gospatric, of a toft with five acres of land in Allithwaite, along with an acre of meadow and pasture for ten cows.[14] This benefaction undoubtedly was intended to provide invaluable shelter and sustenance for members and associates of the abbey passing to and fro between Furness and the south.

The only major territorial gift recorded in Cartmel priory's foundation charter was the area afterwards traditionally known as "the Ancient Parish of Cartmel". This stretched from half-way up the east side of Windermere, along the side of the River Leven and on round the sea coast to the Winster and thence along the border of Westmorland – a very neatly defined unit. Economically this estate was far from rich. The limestone crags of Hampsfell on the east were very barren though there was a little good land along their base. The hills on the western side were mostly of next to no agricultural importance, except in the Walton area and neither was the marshland which linked them to the Leven estuary. Nearby, however, was the very useful quarry of Quarryflat whence came the stone from which the priory was built. In the central area was some better though not extensive land, across which ran the River Ay, a watercourse which was useful but very far from being grandiose.

15

At the time of the foundation of the priory there was in the valley only one sizeable private estate – that of Hampsfield, a well-situated place with a much better water supply than most others in the area. Just before the monastery came into existence, the so-called manor of Hampsfield was granted by King Henry II to a seneschal and it remained in lay hands thereafter. In 1417 an interesting inquisition, or official enquiry, into its boundaries was undertaken, of which full details have survived.[15] Soon after this, it passed to medieval Cartmel's sole knightly family, the Thornboroughs, of whom several mementoes have survived, notably the representation of Sir William Thornborough and his wife in the medieval stained glass in the east window of Bowness parish church.

There cannot be the slightest doubt that the inhabitants of the land of Cartmel in medieval times were mostly small tenant farmers and labourers who were too few and too short of superfluous wealth to contribute more than slightly to the resources of the far from plutocratic priory that stood in their midst.

A royal confirmation of 1215[16] shows us that the new monastery had acquired some minor early possessions – the land of Humphrey Head given by Gilbert of Bolton, part of the pool "which was called Kirkpool" (almost certainly nearby) and an area of land in two tofts with the crofts pertaining to them in "Melsamebi" (wherever that was); two acres in "Estredholme" (another unidentifiable placename) from Alan fitz Ketel, two acres of land in "Bothel" and pasture for eight beasts and two horses, (which may have been intended for a little hostel) at Bolton by Sands. In 1245 a piece of land called Flemingfield and land in Newton was acquired from Peter de Coupland.[17] Before 1315 the priory had obtained "Winterthwaite" from Adam of that name (probably near Witherslack), Ketilseat from Ralph de Winder, Raven Winder and "Madonscales" in the vill of Broughton from Ellis de Staveley.[18] In 1347 William de Kernotteby gave the priory "certain lands in Broughton and Cartmel" in part satisfaction of a previous transaction.[19] Eight years earlier Robert de Walton gave the priory a carucate of land "in Holker in Kertmell"[20] All these were very minor territories which were probably quickly incorporated with existing priory property and so lost their identity. According to an inquest of 1292 the right to a market at Cartmel existed in the time of William Marshall.[21]

The only sizeable local temporal possession which the priory possessed elsewhere consisted of a moiety (or half) of the manor of Silverdale with its appurtenances, given before 1199 by Henry de Redmayne[22] whose original, not very practical, intention had been to bestow it on the far-off little Staffordshire nunnery of Farewell. To this Henry added Haweswater with as much fishing as necessary in his part of this small water, salt cotes and "iron mines" if they were found in the aforesaid land.[23] This place, to which was probably added a few minor pieces, was sufficiently sizeable to support "the cell of Silverdale" which is mentioned in the papal bull of 1233.[24] In 1346 the priory had a messuage and ten acres in Hest[25] and it also had a toft in Bolton given by Adam, son of Gilbert de Bolton.[26] In Whittington for a while it had a little land but exchanged it for some in Allithwaite.[27] As we shall see, on the eve of the Dissolution the priory had rents coming in from Silverdale and Bolton which must have been quite useful, even if far from being substantial. It is likely that, at least for a time, the priory had a little property in Lancaster, which was both the judicial centre of the region and the one major shopping area in the district. In 1309 the prior was claiming a messuage there.[28] In 1444 the prior claimed two acres of land from Roger Rye of Halton.[29] The priory owned next to no property in Furness, very largely because of the huge royal abbey founded there in 1127 which was given, or bought, so much of the limited property available. For a time at least the priory engaged in a little iron-working here, though in 1236 it made legal acknowledgement that it could only do this with the licence of the abbey of Furness.[30] Cartmel did not own anything in South Cumberland.

In the Cartmel area at one time or another the priory acquired what were probably (by the low local standards) comparatively large farms. It seems likely that of these the oldest was Walton Hall where the priory had property in 1342[31] The priory also held Raven Winder,[32] and Canon Winder was acquired at an early but uncertain date.[33] In 1526 the prior leased out Mireside.[34] In pre-Dissolution days Cark was of microscopic importance, and its noble hall was not begun before Elizabethan times. On a little headland on the Leven estuary, where the priory had fishing rights, it erected what a deed of 1545-6 calls "Frith Hall grange", showing us its *raison d'être*.[35] Round the corner, down the coast was the quarry at Quarry Flat from which came most of the building stone for the priory church, a fact locally remembered even in quite recent days, though the quarry has long been derelict and the water on which the stone was anciently transported, cut off by the railway embankment. A rental of the priory's possessions of 1535-6 gives a systematic list of them at that time in the following areas:[36]

(1) *First Account* (8 membranes)
Cark and Holker; Broughton; Aynsome; Templand; Hazelrigg with Ayside; Newton; Grange with Kents Bank; Flookburgh; Flookburgh burgages; Walton; Cartmel Fell; Staveley; (Bailiwick of Silverdale – Silverdale, Hest and Bolton); Cartmel rectory; site of the priory and desmesne lands.

(2) *Bailiwick of Cartmel Fell with members* (3 membranes)
Cartmel Fell (rents, service, silver, custom); "Litterburne" (?Ludder-burne) and "Wayryddynges"; Rosthwaite and "Rullesburgh"; Thorpansty in Cartmel Fell; Tower Wood in Cartmel Fell; "Pullhouse" in

Cartmel Fell; Staveley Mill; Backbarrow mill;

(3) *Bailiwick of Broughton with members* (6 membranes)
Broughton with members; (Broughton – a custom called "les knowinges"); "Avande" in Ayside, Ayside, Seatle and Hazelrigg; – Newton; Lindale; Hampsfell; Birkby; Lindale; Kents Bank; Templand; Greenbank and Aynsome; Aynsome Mill; Seatle; Mireside; Flookburgh; Flookburgh and Cark; Humphrey Head; Cannon Winder; Raven Winder; "Shepesakes" in Kents Bank; Honeythwaite in Kents Bank; Allithwaite mill.

(4) *Bailiwick of Walton and Barngarth with members* (4 membranes)
Walton; "Agyryste" and "Leygryste" in Holker; Holker Mill; Cark and Holker; Quarry Flat; Cartmel (shops in town); Barngarth; the Frith (sale, rent, turbary); Ellerside (turf in Barnmoss etc.); Wastholme moors (turbary); Bigland moss, fishery in the sea etc.

Fishing Rights

MEAT BEING SCARCE and expensive in these parts as well as barred from the monastic diet on no few days in the year, made Cartmel priory's fairly extensive fishing rights of considerable value. The main one of these derived from its possession of the strip of coastline which formed the southern boundary of the "land of Cartmel". This gave the monastery rights over the valuable fishing in the Kent estuary whose water, then as now, harboured *inter alia* the the highly prized salmon. However, similar rights were enjoyed by the lords of Beetham, who owned the corresponding strip of coastline on the south side of the bay. Understandably, the relationship of these two privileges had to be classified by a law-suit. In 1207 the prior sued Ralph de Beetham for obstructing his house's fishing rights.[37] A joint jury from locals in Lancashire and Westmorland was summoned to report on the matter and in 1208 a settlement was reached. Ralph admitted that "the priory and church of St. Michael of Cartmel" had the right they claimed, and the rights of the two parties were defined in an interesting and inevitably rather complex document which incidentally shows that the Kent, then as in these days, had the restless habit of shifting its channel from one part of the estuary to another. It was laid down that when it was on the south side and the tide left pools "lying close to the land and crags" on the Beetham side, the fishing rights were to belong to the lords of that area, but when the position was similar on the north side, fishing rights belonged to the priory. However "when the water lies upon the sand so that men can pass between land and water over either side" fishing was to be "common throughout and for all, both to the prior and his successors and to Ralph and his heirs, down to the sea."[38]

In 1293 John de Lancaster yielded to the priory the right of free fishery in Helton tarn which the prior had claimed in the King's court. He granted the house right to fish there at all times of the year, to draw their boat ashore and secure it on his land on the Witherslack side as well as on their own, and to dry their nets there, though the grantor should have similar rights. In return the priory was to insert on its martyrology the names of the grantor, his wife, his parents and his brother Roger.[39] At an early stage – perhaps at the time of its foundation – the priory acquired useful fishing rights in Windermere.[40]

Spiritual Possessions

THERE IS NO doubt that the major source of Cartmel priory's revenue was that which came from its tenure of the rectory of the parish, which entitled it to the quite extensive tithes, and which, as we shall see, at the time of the dissolution of the monasteries provided a large fraction of its total income. At the end of the thirteenth century (1291) a massive survey of the wealth of the English Church was made at the behest of Pope Nicholas IV. Herein the rectory of Cartmel was assessed at £46.13s.6d. a sum very much greater than that of most of the neighbouring churches, though surpassed by that of Aldingham.[41] The sprawling area and the very small and much scattered population of the land of Cartmel created a very difficult pastoral problem. The inhabitants of its southern parts lived fairly near the great priory church with its parish altar at which they were legally bound to hear mass, but folk at the Cartmel Fell end were some nine or ten miles away from it. By sound medieval laws a place of worship had to be built and an adequate stipend for a priest to serve it had to be secured before any additional facilities for public worship in such distant areas could be approved.

Significantly the only place where one of these existed at an early date was Flookburgh, through whose single street ran the comparatively popular highway which connected Lancaster and the south with Furness and South Cumberland. Unhappily, next to no evidence regarding the medieval history of Flookburgh remains. The sole documentary evidence concerning the chapel here is found only very shortly before the Reformation – in 1520, when Robert Briggs at Cartmel Fell gave it a small piece of land.[42] A small and isolated piece of archaeological evidence survived which suggests a thirteenth century origin for the chapel – a date likely enough on general grounds. This is a voussoir with dog-tooth ornament which may have formed part of the head of the church's main doorway: fifty years ago it sat outside the vicarage door, but has since decamped. Flookburgh chapel stood in the rectangular plot of land which now forms an open square in the village. It was completely rebuilt in 1776-7 but this new structure was totally demolished when the present church of Flookburgh was built on a new site in 1900; the walled-in churchyard remained until 1920 when it too was completely destroyed. In medieval times the small but steady flow of travellers through the village must have provided a trickle of alms to augment the doubtless slim salary of the priest who served it. This chapel had, of course, no right to bury its local adherents, the corpses of these having to be taken to Cartmel for this. The road then taken was that from the bottom of Flookburgh via the Green and Birkby, which came to be traditionally known as the Corpse Road.[43] The place was very poor – as late as 1650 a survey noted that the Flookburgh area had 128 families but its chapel had "neither Minister nor Maintenance."[44]

The only other major place of worship in the land of Cartmel in medieval times was the little chapel set up at Cartmel Fell not very long before the dissolution of the monasteries. In this area the number of inhabitants was certainly sparse, but the flourishing local wool trade centred on Kendal produced one or two of those wealthy families so rare in the area, notably that of the Briggs who lived at Swallowmire. The chapel is mentioned in the will of Robert Briggs, wherein he bequeathed to Cartmel priory a chalice and a "pese" (? a pax) which at Easter was to be lent "to housel with at the chapel of Cartmel Fell". He also gave an annual stipend of 33s.4d. a year for life to John Holme, the priest there, on condition that he took no wages from the hamlet of Cartmel Fell and that he prayed for the souls of his benefactors. Thomas Briggs was to give him his board.[45] Almost certainly the chapel had only very recently been built and providentially it yet retains much of its original fittings. Most interesting are the now somewhat damaged panels of stained glass on the original east window, showing the crucified Christ with scarlet rays from

Cartmel Fell Church

20

**Right:
Mass ordination
rood figure
Cartmel Fell
Church.**

**Left:
Crucifix figure
Cartmel Fell
Church.**

His wounds leading to panels that originally depicted the Seven Sacraments. Of these, Baptism and Confirmation are lost, as are most of Confession and Extreme Unction, but of those of Ordination, Marriage and the Mass there are very extensive remains, the latter being particularly illuminating.[46] Very unusual indeed is the survival here of the major part of a wooden crucifix of pre-Reformation date, which surmounted the original rood screed screen of the chapel. It has very recently been most scientifically restored[47] and at the time of writing is on exhibition in the Kendal Museum. A substantial part of the rood screen

21

itself was re-used to make the large family pew pertaining to the family at Cowmire Hall, which stands at the east end of the nave on the north side. Unhappily, we have next to no evidence concerning the early chaplains who served the chapel.

Brief mention of several very minor ecclesiastical units in the Cartmel area may be made here. It is quite likely that St. Andrew's Moor, just above Hampsfield, takes its name from a chantry chapel dedicated to this saint and perhaps founded by the well-to-do Thornborough family which lived at the nearby hall. If so, it would be well placed by the cross roads north of the priory to attract some little attention and alms from passers-by. A report of 1527 notes *inter alia* "there is a chapel upon the north side of the town of Cartmel which (was) edified in the honour and worship of Mary Magdalene and is now in decay."[48] This is the sole reference to such a chapel, as far as we know, and may be erroneous as St. Andrew's moor is nearby.

Further afield, by a deed of 1275-90 William of Stirkeland confirmed to the priory of Cartmel perpetual care and custody of the chapel of Crosscrake, formerly founded by Anselm, son of Michael of Furness, in the grantor's territory of Stainton in Kendal, with its lands and possessions and control of the chapel and its goods. The priory, says the deed, should appoint a priest to the chapel to celebrate divine service for the grantor's ancestors and successors but none of the latter's heirs should distrain the prior or his chaplain to receive any lepers or infirm at the chapel against their will or to support or render hospitality to them.[49] The priory itself can have derived little or no advantage from its rights here. Concerning other properties, there are slight indications that the priory owned a little chantry at Hest[50] and the advowson of the church at Whittington was claimed by the priory as having been given them in the time of King John. In 1300 the patrons were prepared to concede it, but opposition by a local jury led to the claim being abandoned, and despite further investigation in 1334 the sole advantage to the priory established herein was a pension of 4 marks.[51] Near it was a hermitage of which next to nothing is known.

As was usual, once the monastery had taken firm root it acquired a major papal confirmation of the house's ecclesiastical possessions and privileges which has happily survived. It was granted in 1233 by Gregory IX[52] and shows that the priory's main ecclesiastical possessions (in England) were then "the priory site", "the church of St. Michael of Kermel" (the old parish church which probably had not yet been structurally replaced by the new priory church) and the cell of "Sellredale" (evidently a short-lived settlement on the site at Silverdale given by Henry of Redmayne).

The Irish Connection

WILLIAM MARSHALL'S WIFE Isabel had inherited considerable possessions in Ireland, and it is worthy of note that he founded no less than three monasteries there – the Cistercian abbey of Tintern Parva (1200) in gratitude for being saved from drowning at sea, another house of the same order at Graiguenamanagh about 1207 and a hospital at Kilkenny about 1201-2, which soon after became a house of Austin canons.[53] To Cartmel priory the Earl gave the church of Ballysax with the chapel of Ballymaden and the vill and advowson of Kilrush (Co. Kildare),[54] where Cartmel established a cell. The fact that Cartmel priory's Irish possessions were so very distant from it made it essential to seek a *pied-à-terre* reasonably close to them and accounts for the fact that at a very early date (1200) the house made an arrangement with the Austin canons of Dublin cathedral (Holy Trinity) whereby the latter undertook to provide hospitality for visiting Cartmel brethren in need thereof, and also undertook to celebrate requiems for deceased brethren of the priory, and to include their names in the martyrology of their house.[55] A little later we find the canons of St. Thomas, Dublin disputing Cartmel's title to the church of Ballysax and the chapel of Ballymaden, but in 1205 they relinquished their claim in return for compensation.[56]

Although Cartmel's Irish possessions were far from princely they were quite useful, especially because of the infertility of much of Cartmel soil and the priory's none too easy task of acquiring cereals for that daily bread which was the staple diet of medieval England. In 1208 King John had granted the priory permission to purchase necessaries in Ireland and import them, free of toll, following permission to purchase corn there.[57] Similar royal licences followed in 1236 and 1240 for the import of 200 crannocks of wheat from Kilross.[58] In 1322, probably because of recent ferocious raids by the Scots, Holm Cultram abbey and Cartmel priory were granted royal protection for two years for the men they were sending to Ireland to buy corn and other victuals for their own maintenance.[59]

From the late thirteenth century onwards for a bare hundred years we have interesting data regarding the appointments made by the priory of legal representatives in Ireland. These often seem to have been two in number; one a canon, the other a layman. In 1292 these were the canon Thomas of York and Gilbert of Walton who had royal protection for two years.[60] In 1299 brother Henry of Huberslack and Roger le Waleys were appointed,[61] in 1310 William of Alyngthwaite, a canon, and Roger le Waleys again.[62] In 1312 the prior of Cartmel appointed Robert de Burge and Robert, son of William de Gaytsum to be his attorneys in Ireland i.e. legal representatives there.[63] Four years previously William of Nottingham (wrongly described as the prior's "fellow monk") and Alexander Waleys were made attorneys in Ireland for two years,[64] and in 1315

William le Surrays (a canon) and William of Lindale were appointed for the same period.[65] In 1317 William was re-appointed along with Simon le Horsnave.[66] In 1319 the nominees were William of Nottingham again and William of Oxclif:[67] in 1347 Adam of Poulton, a canon, and William of Bredek:[68] in 1353 Richard of Kellott, a canon, and Adam Ellotesson:[69] in 1355 Thomas Brown, a lay brother and Robert le Waleys:[70] in 1357 Thomas Brown a canon, and Robert Waleys:[71] in 1361 Thomas Browne and John de Bolton canons:[72] in 1357 Thomas Brown canon and Thomas de Chaumbre:[73] in 1380 Robert de Greves, a canon and Thomas Ryner:[74] in 1392 Thomas de Morthyng and Thomas Haver for three years.[75] Why the list of attorneys does not continue into the fifteenth century is not clear.

Very little indeed is known about the history of Cartmel priory's cell of Kilrush, but I am much obliged to Professor MacNeil of the University of Ireland for drawing my attention to the following useful evidence hereon. In 1263 the priory leased to archbishop Fulco of Dublin the rights and revenue of their manor of Kilrush and its church for a period of six years for a sum of £50 a year to be paid in two instalments. The archbishop was to be responsible for the maintenance in good order of the site of the manor with its buildings, gates, gardens, fishponds, dovecotes and close (*clausura*), and also to make provision for the canon of Cartmel appointed as proctor by the priory and for two horses and grooms.[76] A survey of 1264 shows that there were at Kilross 244½ acres of which 90 were sown with corn and hastiber and 35 acres of grassland.[77] The prior at this time was one Roger who was in Ireland with Peter his superior and three other canons – Geoffrey of Treske, William of Kendal and William of Asfordeby.[78]

A revealing little survey of Cartmel priory's property in Ireland at the time of the Dissolution has survived, made in 28 Hen. VIII (1536-7).[79] It details that in the manor of Kilrush was a castle and a small garden, of no little worth except for the use of the farmer. There were 360 acres of land of which 60 had long been uncultivated. The other 300 were held by 6 tenants and were worth 12d. an acre, thus producing £15. There were 11 cottagers on the estate who paid no dues but were bound to undertake two days' labour in the autumn. (All the tenants were each bound to render a cock valued at 2d at Christmas.) The total income was £16.4s.6d. The tithes of the rectory of Kilrush were worth 66s.2d and the altarage 20s, besides the portion allotted to the vicar. To it pertained a water mill assessed at 10s. and an old dovecote worth 2s. The patronage and advowson belonged to the Crown, being part of the manor. There were no villeins. The total value was £6.6s.8d.

Internal Life

PERENIALLY THERE IS usually little for the historian to note concerning the internal life of a monastery. In the Augustinian order to which Cartmel priory belonged the bretheren's day was largely engrossed by the maintenance of a complex but uneventful round of service which began in the early hours of the morning and, after a break of several hours, continued off and on throughout the day until darkness. Although Austin canons were legally entitled to undertake duties at the parish altars which pertained to their house, it seems unlikely that at Cartmel this permission was very extensively used, since it was incompatible with full attendance at the complex liturgical round of their monastic regime and the number of brethren were not large. As we have seen, a very small trickle of brethren visited the priory's establishment at Ballsax for brief periods. Two misfortunes prevent us knowing much about the common life at Cartmel. Firstly, the priory was situate in the arch-diocese of York, whose very busy holders had little contact with it. Quickly and understandably, these most important and hardworked prelates unloaded most of the routine work in the far-distant western part of their area, on the arch-deacons of Richmond, in whose sphere North Lonsdale and South Cumberland were included, and whose medieval archives have almost completely vanished. In 1233 the longish bull of pope Gregory VIII had granted the privileges usual when a new monastery had been effectively established, to "the church of the Holy Mother of God, the Virgin Mary of Cartmel", but also forbade the system of election of a prior laid down in the foundation charter. It specifically laid down that the head of the community should be chosen "by common consent" or the majority of brethren of an upper council.[80] The foundation charter's provision for the patrons of the priory to have a slight but direct say in choice of a new prior having been thus explicitly banned by the pope, there followed in 1250 a final concord whereby the patrons of the priory recognised this in law. Joan de Valence and her husband agreed with the brethren of the priory that when the office of prior was vacant, the latter should seek permission from the patrons to proceed to an election, but should have complete freedom of choice, though during the vacancy the patron should be entitled to have maintained at the priory, at its charge, one servant with two horses and two grooms; this servant and the cellarer of the house should ensure that during the vacancy "the canons, brethren and servants" of the place should be supplied with all the necessaries without waste or destruction.[81]

In 1229 had been recorded a useful glimpse of the slender means of the priory, at a stage when its building programme was almost certainly in poor straits, when Archbishop Walter Grey granted an indulgence of 20 days to the faithful who aided with their alms the priory of Cartmel, whose possessions were said to be so insignificant that they were scarcely adequate for the canons dwelling there to support their guests.[82] A little later came one of the very few indications in the history of the priory that the standard of behaviour there was in such need of improvement that high-level intervention was necessary. A papal document of 1245 shows that an unspecified number of canons and lay brothers of the priory had been excommunicated for using personal violence on each other, retaining private property, refusing to obey their prior and, in certain cases, of celebrating divine worship when excommunicate. The prior was now authorised to grant absolution and dispense the less heinous offenders provided they were penitent, to suspend the unrepentant for two years and send to Rome for absolution those guilty of violence.[83] However, this was evidently not the end of the matter for three years later the abbot of Furness and the provost of Beverley were authorised to enquire into alleged misbehaviour at Cartmel and remove the prior from office if this seemed necessary.[84] The result of this inquest is not known.

As far as we know at present, only one medieval archbishop of York carried out the very lengthy and unpleasant journeying which an official visitation of the South Cumbrian portion of his grossly over-large arch-diocese involved. This was arch-bishop William Wickwane who on 2 May 1281, after carrying out at the priory the lengthy and complex investigation usual in such cases, issued to its brethren a series of injunctions.[85] He ordered, first, that the prior and his brethren should not, as hitherto, break the strict rules regarding silence in their régime, but strictly observe them. They were to be careful not to admit "secular and worthless people" into the infirmary, refectory or cloister. It was very strictly forbidden for any canon to converse during the time of the claustral procession with any woman; if such conversation should be necessary, the prior or presiding cannon should invariably listen to what was being said. The statutes associated with the *Rule* (of St. Augustine) were to be faithfully and firmly observed. The prior's aid assigned to the building fund of the church was to be profitably utilised for that purpose, to the extent and as often as could be conveniently arranged, lest local folk (*compatriote*) withdrew the customary approbation. The entrance to the cloisters were to be more strictly guarded than hitherto customary against strangers. Those in priests' orders were to celebrate masses according to decree of the rules and canons, as often they have an undefiled and pure conscience. Totally forbidden because of 'certains for evil' was the presence of any woman in the claustral procession. Any canon who retained a saddle and the other equipment for riding was to immediately hand them over to the prior so that they could be issued to the canons when needed, by the prior or his deputy. All canons were forbidden to leave the cloister without the permission of the prior or president of the cloister, most especially from love of hunting, but also for any other reason, unless necessary and the due permission for this departure could be pleased.

Soon after, a further visitation was announced for March 1294 by Archbishop le Romeyn, but his ill-health and other trouble led to its cancellation.[86] In 1355 William of Nottingham canon of Cartmel was one of many who acquired papal permission to choose a confessor who would give him if penitent, plenary remission of sins at the hour of his death.[87] In 1391 William prior of Cartmel and in 1396 another canon of the house, John of Aldingham, acquired the same right.[88] A little later, as we shall see, came a report which, probably unreliably, cast aspersions on the then prior.

By a decree of the Fourth Lateran Council of 1215 the Austin canons, like some other monastic orders, were obliged to hold periodic general chapters organised on a local basis. Those for England began in 1217[89] with one at Leicester to which all heads of independent houses were summoned. But the fact that there were now almost two hundred houses of Austin canons here, very widely scattered over the country made this arrangement intolerably unwieldy, given the slowness of medieval travel. Probably in 1220 or in 1223 it was agreed that houses in the provinces of Canterbury and York should hold separate chapters though even this must have been a trying arrangement, for in the case of the latter most of its northern houses were situated in remote spots like Cartmel, Conishead, Carlisle, Lanercost and Brinkburn. They were far apart since the huge province only contained twenty houses. In 1337 the pope ordered the two general chapters in England to combine again into a single unit. The decree of all these general chapters of the English Austin canons suggest that, by and large, they were not very useful or very successful. References therein to Cartmel are very scanty. In 1278, at short notice, the prior of Nostell replaced the prior of Cartmel[90] as president for the northern chapter, the reason for the latter's failure to turn up not being noted. At a major chapter at Guisborough in 1285 the prior of Cartmel, like all the rest, accepted the new statutes drawn up to establish unity.[91] In 1404 the prior was an official of the general chapter held at Northampton.[92]

Although evidence concerning the religious life of Cartmel priory is mostly very scanty before this time, such as exists suggests that things were going well, as it certainly was on the eve of the Dissolution. At the end of the fourteenth century, however, the priory life had evidently hit a bad patch, for which the prior at first seems to have received more than his fair share of the blame. In 1392 a papal mandate required the archbishop of York to remove William, prior of Cartmel, if reports were true that he had been guilty of delipidation and spending the proceeds on depraved uses, of simony in admitting men to be professed in the priory, and of frequent visits to taverns so that buildings of the monastery were falling down. It was alleged that divine worship and hospitality were neglected, scandal caused by the prior's dishonest life and the monastery brought to a miserable state.[93] This sort of spectacular accusation was not uncommon in contemporary church life and, like similar ones in certain sections of our press since, need to be treated with caution. With this mandate came another authorising the removal of prior William and the election of a new prior, but the fact that this was not utilised suggests that William was not guilty of any serious misdemeanours, as does the issue to him in 1396 of the right to have a confessor of his own choice who should grant him plenary remission of sins at the hour of his death.[94] The only other serious allegation at this time which was almost certainly sound, claimed that Cartmel's monastic buildings were falling into decay. This was indubitably no new problem but one of long standing.

It is unfortunate that the very scanty evidence on the matter makes it impossible to determine the periods of office of the fifteenth century priors of Cartmel, the problem being made more difficult since there were more than one of them at this time called William. Of one of them however, an extremely interesting mention has come to light comparatively recently in an elaborate and attractively written deed deposited in the County Records Office at Preston. It is directed to prior William of Cartmel by the head of the English province of the Dominicans on its behalf, and expresses immense gratitude to him for certain help which must have been considerable but the nature of which, most unfortunately, is recorded only in very abstract terms. It mentions "your devotion which you have towards our Order" and promises the prior in return extensive spiritual services after his death, showing him in this respect the same privileges as if he had been a member of their order. The document is dated on the feast of the Assumption (14 Aug.) 1418.[95] It is very probable that this prior William had been instrumental in securing for the Dominicans a substantial bequest from the estate of the recently deceased Lord William Harrington.

As is much too often the case, very little information about the size of the monastic community has survived. At the time of its foundation, houses having a prior and twelve Austin canons, (in imitation of Christ and the twelve apostles), were very common, and it may well be this was Cartmel's original size though it cannot be proved. The first certain evidence shows that there were seven brethren in 1381.[96] In 1536 at the time of the Dissolution, the number of brethren was ten, as we shall see.[97]

The very remote situation of Cartmel and the immense difficulty of reaching it, inevitably meant that very few lay dignitaries came this way in medieval times. The pious "lord Edward" (later Kind Edward I) possibly visited the priory at St. Bees and what may be faint memories of his visit linger on in Flookburgh through which he may have passed. The only medieval king of England who is at all likely to have seen the priory is the unfortunate King Henry VI, who, after defeat in battle wandered pathetically about Cumbria and North Lancashire. He certainly visited Muncaster and Furness abbey, and may well have visited Cartmel, though of this we have no proof.

Secular Matters

AT THE TIME that Cartmel priory was founded what were to become the county boundaries of north-western England had recently been established. The Cartmel and Furness areas were assigned to Lancashire probably largely through the desirability of having both sides of the over-sands route under a single local legal authority.

However, the obstreperous and scantily provided Scots were never ready to accept the official frontier in those days, and, from time to time, launched raids on northern England which left behind no little death and destruction of property, notably of the cereals which were the main source of contemporary food. Some of these raids swept down the Eden valley where communications were easy and the local inhabitants less indigent than their neighbours who lived to the west. But on two major occasions during the history of our priory the Scots took our locals by surprise and attacked Lancashire north of the Sands.

In 1316, as the *Lanercost Chronicle* records, the Scots came over from Richmond "laying waste everything as far as Furness, and burnt that district whither they had not come before, taking away with them nearly all the goods of that district, with men and women as prisoners. Especially were they delighted with the abundance of iron which they found there".[98] To make matters worse, this year saw in England and Scotland "such famine and pestilence as had not been heard of in our time". Six years later Robert de Brus renewed this attack. This time the Scottish king took the little used coastal route. After plundering the abbey of Holm Cultram ("notwithstanding that his father's body was buried there"), he proceeded across the Duddon sand to Furness where the very well-to-do abbey bribed him (doubtless heavily) to ensure that this monastery "should not again be burnt or plundered..."[99] This notwithstanding, the Scots set fire to various places and lifted spoils. They then went further, beyond the sands of Leven to Cartmel and "burnt the lands round the priory of black canons taking away cattle and spoil; and so they crossed the sands of Kent as far as Lancaster". The extent of the damage wrought by these incursions need not be assessed purely by the imagination, for contemporary official statistics are available. The value of the temporalities of Cartmel which has been assessed at £21.11s.8d. in the *Taxation of Pope Nicholas* of 1292 were reduced to £3.6s.8d. in the new taxation,[100] and that of its spiritualities from £46.13s.4d. to

29

£8.0s.0d.[101]

Towards the end of the fifteenth century, for the first and last time in their history, Furness and Cartmel (albeit briefly) hit the headlines of national news. On 4 June 1487 the upstart Lambert Simnel and certain malcontent nobles, with some two thousand German mercenaries and hordes of ill-equipped Irishmen, landed from Ireland at Peel castle to prosecute his very bogus claim to the English throne against the newly-established Henry VII. As the Parliament Rolls quaintly put it – "there arrived a great navie in Furness in Lancashire...accompanied with a great multitude of strangers with force and armes, that is to saye, swerdis, speris, mares spikes, bowes, gounes, harneys, brigandines, hawberkes, and many other wepins and harneys defencible".[102] Amongst the first to join the invaders were two local gentry, Sir Thomas Broughton of Broughton Towers and James and Thomas Harrington, younger members of that great local family which held *inter alia* Aldingham, Gleaston and lands in the Hornby area. But their rash venture soon ended in total failure at the battle of Stoke-on-Trent. Local tradition, here so often accurate in these matters, maintains that Sir Thomas Broughton, being of course a traitor, went into hiding somewhere in the Witherslack area, where he still had land and friends, and died there, his body being buried somewhere in the vicinity. Quickly, after the rapid collapse of the revolt, a group of knights were empowered by the Crown to "admit into the King's Grace and allegiance, all rebels in Furness fells, Cartmel and the precincts thereof" who were willing to submit, these were pardoned by letters under the great seal.[103]

The Latter Days of the Monastery

IN THE CENTURY that preceded the dissolution of Cartmel priory, there was probably little of more than domestic interest to record. Certainly documentary evidence is far from rich. It is known that a major crisis arose over the priory buildings. In the last decade of the fourteenth century it was asserted that monastic buildings at Cartmel were in ruin and, as we shall see, existing architectural remains show that very extensive rebuilding took place in the following sixty years. This included the replacement of the original very inadequate nave by the present one which, though very far from being palatial, was a major improvement on its predecessor. Also belonging to this period was the very complex and surprising replacement of the original cloister court and its attendant buildings which nestled against the south side of the church, by an entirely new set of those on the opposite, (northern) side. New cloisters, chapter house, refectory dormitory and probably the prior's lodgings

Left:
Cartmel Priory -
Arms of the monastery

Right:
Cartmel Priory -
Canopy in the East Window

Cartmel Priory - East Window
i) an Archbishop   ii) a female martyr iii) head of God the Father

were all erected here. The expense and inconvenience which this rebuilding involved must have been immense. There seems to be no known case of any other of the thousand monasteries of medieval England undertaking a similar very radical transformation.

What was the reason for Cartmel so doing? To this question, almost certainly there can be only one answer – the fact that the foundations of the cloisters and its attendant buildings had turned out to be totally unsuitable, so that the structures on it were in a state of decay, as the charges against Prior William had recently declared, though of course, the prior himself had little or no responsibility for this state of things. The reason of this move was probably a geological one. As Dr Murray Mitchell has pointed out, the area in and around the village of Cartmel is one of remarkable complexity, with no less than five different kinds of stone within quite a small radius. The church itself, like the gate-house and nearby houses, stands very securely on Bannisdale slate, all of them to this day showing no signs of instability. But the original cloister site (not that part of the cemetery which adjoins the south side of the nave), stood on foundations which proved very inadequate when subjected to the stress of massive cloister buildings. What was almost completely new was the present nave with all its windows, and also the remarkable belfry tower set diagonally across the old lantern, thus giving the priory a feature which is unique in England. One result of this extensive transference of the conventual buildings was to leave a large open space on the south side of the church which, along with adjoining land to the south, must at this time have been consecrated as a cemetery for the parishioners, a function for which its situation was ideally suited: (it is quite likely that part of this area had previously been used as the private cemetery for brethren of the monastery).

Although stylistic architectural evidence gives us a very approximate date for this great building operation at Cartmel, it is unfortunate and a little surprising that so far no very precise documentary evidence concerning it has yet been discovered, though two small clues are worthy of note. The great east window of the priory with what was originally inserted as part of the massive re-building programme and its mighty panoply of glass has been dated by Dr Peter Newton to about the third decade of the fifteenth century.[104] Further, amongst the heraldic glass from Cartmel priory (now in the east window of Bowness parish church) is the coat of arms of Lord Grey of Ruthen quartering Hastings and Valence. This peer had inherited the position of legal patron of the priory and as such would have certainly been expected to have contributed handsomely towards the cost of any major restoration there. He acquired his barony in 1388 and died in 1440, a period which perfectly coincides with the architectural features of the new work in the chancel. Some, though by no means all, of the other coats-of-arms in this fascinating window of Bowness, probably belong to donors who subscribed towards the very heavy expense of this restoration of the priory.

Of the religious activity of the priory in these times few points of any interest are known. In Feb. 1399 Richard of Bolton, the prior of Conishead and Edmund Eslake were commissioned to carry out a visitation of the house,[105] but of this nothing further is recorded. In 1430 the prior of Cartmel was commissioned to undertake the enclosure of one Alice Skawesby "in a certain dwelling built for anchorites alongside the church of Kirkby Kendal".[106] In 1467 the then prior of Cartmel was similarly authorised to receive the vow of continence and chastity from "the honourable and devout woman Dowce", relict of Walter Strickland, squire, late of the parish of Kirkby in Kendal deceased, in order that she may be able the more securely and devoutly to do service to her Maker.[107]

Of the work of the priors of Cartmel at this time little is known. As we have seen, various complaints made against prior William Lawrence who had been elected in 1381, reached the pope,[108] but they were probably exaggerated as he was not removed from office. Amongst them, as we noted, was blame for buildings of the priory then being in disrepair, which was certainly not his fault. At the end of the fifteenth century came more domestic trouble though not of major proportions. Prior William Hale was removed from office by Christopher Urswick, the archdeacon of Richmond, for alleged "excesses", but seems to have successfully appealed against this sentence. In 1501 he sought to secure the return to the house of two canons who had left for an unknown period and an unknown reason.[109] The penultimate prior, James Grigg, confessed on his death-bed that he had lent £70 of the house's money to certain persons, one of whom was a relative.[110] In 1518 at the general chapter of the Austin canons at Leicester it was reported that one of Cartmel's canons, William Panell, had apostasised;[111] at the Dissolution it was recorded that he was 68 and had been given a pension and leave to live where he pleased by the convent.[112] However, the ordeal of the Dissolution brought out very strongly the fact that the morale of the brethren of Cartmel priory was then very high, and their devotion to the monastic life very strong.

A very useful list of secular clergy in the archdeaconry of Richmond in 1524[113] gives us their names and the amount of their assessment for ecclesiastical taxation. Under Cartmel it records first Oliver Levyns (the canon in spiritual charge of the parish) £5.6s.8d., along with no less than nine other chaplains viz: John Levyns (perhaps a relation of Oliver), Walter Pepper, Thomas Barker and Christopher Berry (all £1.6s.8d), followed by James Berrey (£2), Nyles Hinde (£1) Roger Knype (£2), John Holme (£4) and Edward Mychellson (£3.6s.8d). One would like to know the duties and posts of each. The last two may have been better paid than the rest through being attached to the chantry of Lord John and Lady

Joan Harrington; two of the others would be needed to serve the chapels at Flookburgh and Cartmel Fell.

An early, large seal of the priory in the British Museum, shows Our Lady seated with the infant Christ on her right knee, and a sceptre with a bird on top in her left hand, between the two small saltire crosses. On the reverse is shown St. Michael (to whom the pre-existing church at Cartmel had been dedicated) and his dragon. Another smaller and rather later seal shows Our Lady full length, crowned, with a sceptre in her right hand and a book in her left.[114] The arms of the priory were *part per pale or et vert, a lion rampant gules*, i.e. a shield divided vertically into gold and green halves over which was imposed a red lion rampant.[115]

The Dissolution

NOTHING IN THE life of the English Church at the opening of the sixteenth century gave the slightest suggestion that very quickly indeed the monastic life, which had been lived steadily for almost a thousand years in not far short of the same number of religious houses, would be rapidly and completely extinguished. The suppression of this much loved institution, out of the blue, came as the arbitrary act of the greedy and sexridden King Henry VIII. The essential first move in the process was a systematic and elaborate survey of all the property of the monasteries in England, the results of which were codified in the massive *Valor Ecclesiasticus* of 1535. The royal officials who visited Cartmel for this purpose produced only a brief, probably hurried report. The subsequent history of the monastery is unusually well-documented and has been fully and magisterially told by Dr C. Haigh.[116]

The priory's main annual income from spiritualities was assessed and came from tithes of one kind or another, including sea fish, and were assessed at £23.10s. to which were added a pension of 53s.4d. from the church of Whittington. The house's temporal assets were its site, gardens, orchards, arable and pasture whose total annual yield was put at £8.16s.6d., rents from property in Cartmel, Silverdale, Bolton and Hest which totalled £78.19s.7d. and some very minor items which added up to a mere 20s. Against this were to be set pensions at 26s.8d. to Conishead priory, and 40s. to two clerks who served in the parish altar at Cartmel along with a number of payments to laity great and small *viz.* 40s. to the Earl of Derby; 33s.4d. to the seneschal of the priory court; £4 to the auditor, William Nelson; £4 to the bailiff of Cartmel, William Byrked; 20s. to the bailiff of Silverdale, Rolland Jakeson; 26s.8d. to the "receiver" of the priory, Peter Byrkhed. With them was recorded the interesting and unusual item of £6 to William Gate, "bailiff and guide (conductor) of all the people of the lord King across the sands of the sea called Cartmel sands, by the foundation of the founder". Finally, is noted an annual payment of 6s.8d. made on Easter Day for "various boys and others" and in alms distributed to seven poor folk who prayed daily for the founder. The total net income was estimated at £91.6s.3d.

Through wickedness or haste or both, this assessment was certainly much too low, so the priory understandably protested against it, as it was the smaller monastic houses which were specially threatened at this time. In Feb. 1536 an Act of Parliament authorised the suppression of all monasteries having a net annual income of less than £200. In June royal officials came to Cartmel and carried out a very much fuller survey[117] increasing the assessment to £212.12s.10½d. For this crucial period we have a complete list of the Austin canons who served it with their full names and ages. These were: Richard Preston, prior (42); James Eskrigge, sub-prior (36); William Pannell (68); Richard Backhouse (41); John Ridley, formerly cellarer (32); Augustine Fell (33); Thomas Briggs (30); Thomas Person (25); Brian Willan (28); John Cowper (25). A very notable feature of this list is the very high proportion of young brethren – always a sign of spiritual vitality.

Also recorded here are ample details of the priory's employees. They number 37 and carried out a number of functions. Attached to the house itself were a baker, a brewer, a barber, a cook, a scullion, and a butler of the refectory. The outside staff comprised two woodsmen, a keeper of the woods, two millers, a fisherman, a wright, a poulterer, a "foster man", a malt maker, two shepherds and a hunter. At first sight this staff may seem numerous, but it is to be remembered that this was in an age when the monastery had to be effectively self-supporting and had a large number of non-monastic mouths to feed, including the poor and what was certainly a steady flow of travellers of one kind or another, to whom the priory was expected to offer hospitality. In an area where towns and hostels were non-existent, small and scattered inns alone offered accommodation for strangers. Dr Haigh quotes a curious contemporary document showing the great value of monastic hospitality in northern parts to "strangers and baggers of corn as betwixt Yorkshire, Lancashire, Kendal, Westmorland and the Bishopric"[118] (of Durham). The same writer shows irrefutably that northern monasticism "was still integrated in the life of the country and performed important functions and point out "the average proportion of annual income devoted to almsgiving in the monasteries (of England) was about 2½%" but here was 7.6%.[119] He notes further that "Lancashire monasteries in fact appear to have acted as unofficial bankers for the area and that the prior of Cartmel was greatly friended and favoured".[120] Following the Act of Suppression came a host of individual surrenders by totally helpless monasteries, royal policy hereon inspiring no little hatred and opposition, principally in Lincolnshire and northern parts – notably Yorkshire. At an uncertain date in the autumn Cartmel priory was closed down. But in October there broke out, especially in Lincolnshire and Yorkshire a vigorous and quite widespread revolt in favour of the monasteries, in the course of which the old régime was restored in several of them. At Cartmel this happened in October, all the brethren returning there, though the prior, lacking confidence or courage, sought and acquired Crown protection from the Earl of Derby at Preston. For some time the whole situation seemed in the melting pot with few hopeful signs. Then early in December the Vicar-General wrote to the brethren at Cartmel and those of Conishead (who had also been re-instated) to inform them that all religious orders were to return to their houses at the royal behest and expressing the hope that their monasteries should stand for ever.[121] On December 22nd a general pardon for monastic rebels was declared at Kendal.[122]

But some eight weeks later, for purely local reasons, the storm (which was certainly bound to come in the end) broke at Cartmel. A certain Thomas Holcroft, very well in with the right people, and very much interested in feathering his own nest, had acquired for himself, amongst other items of local monastic property, the "farm" of the rectory of Cartmel which gave him the right to claim the priory harvest newly stored in the barns of Barngarth. However, to the locals it seemed reasonable to believe that it was highly improper for him to deprive the legally re-instated brethren of their daily bread. When some of Holcroft's men arrived to do just this a major affray broke out – the only one that Cartmel has ever seen. Inevitably the devout locals, untrained and ill-equipped as they were, were defeated. Some succeeded in escaping, but six canons and sixteen laymen (or 'yeomen' as they were termed) were carried off to prison at Lancaster, where they were put on trial on the serious charge of treason. Under a very recent Act, the law defined this in scandalously wild terms – making it a major penal offence even to "wish, will or desire" harm to the king. They were guilty of violating the royal pardon by resisting the King's lessees.

Two of the canons – Brian Willan and Thomas Briggs – were found not guilty and acquitted, but the other four were found guilty and condemned to a cruel death at Lancaster. They were the very aged William Pannell, Augustine Fell, Richard Backhouse and John Cowper. With them suffered also ten faithful laymen, Peter Barwyck, Matthew Bateman, Robert Dawson, James Carter, John Blackhed, John Bigland, John Brockbank, William Crossefield, William Byrkhead, Gilbert Preston.[123] Of the two canons acquitted, Brian Willan became curate at Cartmel from before 1548 until at least 1585, his will being proved in 1592,[124] whilst Thomas Briggs obtained clerical employment at Ulverston;[125] both of them married. What happened to the now well-to-do ex-prior Richard Preston is not clear and the same is true of James Eskrig and John Ridley,

35

but Thomas Preston pertinaciously made his way to Scotland to become an Austin canon at Holyrood.[126] Three of the yeomen involved, two of them being Miles and John Dicconson (presumably from the Wraysholme family) had escaped capture but John was found in 1539 and his transmission to London ordered.[127]

The Aftermath

THE SUPPRESSION OF the priory at Cartmel clearly brought in its train wide-ranging changes, which need not all be here monitored in detail. The monastic possessions were rented out or sold off in a complex series of transactions most of which can be clearly glimpsed in the calendar of the Holker deeds, now so very conveniently in print. This process was a very complex and piecemeal one which in the new century left most of them in the hands of the junior branch of the Preston family. The elder branch was uncomprisingly Roman Catholic and was entrenched for a century or so at Furness abbey. The Holker branch aided Cartmel church in no small way. In one respect, however, the people of Cartmel were much more fortunate than others living in places where the main church of the area was monastic as well as parochial.

In those churches local folk had traditionally worshipped in the western limb of the church which was preserved for their use when the rest of the building and its contents were hurriedly sold off for what it would fetch at the Dissolution. At Cartmel, however, the parishioners' position was very different and may even have been unique. Here, certainly for financial reasons, a very long while had originally passed before the priory church acquired a sizeable nave, the smallish and poorish congregation of the area making do largely, if not entirely, with the south choir aisle and the south transept, neither of which seem ever to have been reclaimed for conventual use. The monastic community doubtless found the chancel, north choir aisle and north transept quite adequate for its needs – as we have seen, the sparse evidence suggests that the number of brethren was seldom more than a dozen and was sometimes less. As a result the royal officials charged with suppressing the priory found themselves faced with a novel situation regarding which they sought advice from their superiors in a not very well expressed query: "Item for the parish church of Cartmel whether it stand unplucked down or no" to which the answer was made, "Ordered by Mr Chancellor of the Duchy that it stand still".[128] It is not clear how this order is to be squared with the Tait's assertion in the *Victoria County History* that "not content with the south part of the church, which had always been set apart for their use, the parishioners purchased the whole".[129]

It is most unfortunate that for a long while books on the priory have asserted that its church was unroofed at the Dissolution and so remained for eighty years, when Mr George Preston restored it. It is beyond all doubt that there is no good evidence to support this. The *Church Book* does show that some major restoration was undertaken at this time, but examination shows that it was comparatively limited in scope. In 1615 £10 was expended on the leads and roof adjoining the Piper Choir and 20 marks laid out for "casting and mending the leads over the parish (Town) choir" and other repairs.[130] In 1617 it was agreed to raise "two twenty mark castes for repair" at "the two roofes and the steeple" whose repair Mr Preston was undertaking, and two entries the next year show that the roofs concerned were those of the Town Choir, to be built up and made anew and "the other roof over the Ladies Quire and piper choir".[131]

What, in fact, actually happened to the church at the time the monastery was dissolved? Almost certainly, as was usual enough, beginning with the chancel the royal servants started to strip off the lead of the church roof, which had considerable market value and was usually melted down on the spot to be sold elsewhere. But the exceptional arrangement at Cartmel, whereby a substantial part of the eastern limb of the church was parochial property as also, in fact, was the south transept, led to the parish protest noted above, which would have been made without delay and almost certainly stopped this spoilation before it had gone very far. The obvious initial royal target would be the lead on the chancel roof which was indubitably monastic property and may have been wholly or largely removed, perhaps leaving gaping rafters. But it should be noted that there is absolutely no sign of the tops of the walls which supported this roof having been seriously damaged by long exposure to the elements, whilst substantial parts of the elaborate and extensive 15th century choir stalls below the chancel roof are virtually intact. It is true that the elaborate backs and canopies of these have completely gone, but the seats with their exquisite misericords remain in virtually perfect condition, whilst the desks in front of them show only minor signs of damage, except for that of the finials at their bench ends. Almost certainly the damage to the chancel was quickly limited by the official injunction just quoted, and perhaps also by the parishioners quickly erecting temporary protection for the stalls. So far as other parts of the church is concerned, it is to be noted that the north choir aisle had a solid stone vault which shows no sign of damage, whilst there is absolutely no evidence to show that the transepts, crossing and nave ever suffered any harm at this time, almost certainly because they had been mostly the traditional preserve of the local parishioners.

The *Church Book*, from which the worthy Stockdale long ago printed invaluable extracts, shows quite clearly that the roof repair work which Mr George Preston carried out (in the years 1617-22) concerned only the

The interior before the Victorian restoration

The present interior from the east

chancel, Piper Choir and Town Choir, and that the expenses were not so large as to suggest enormous damage had to be remedied. Of his generosity it is impossible to speak too highly. Not only was he largely, though not wholly, responsible for putting the church in good repair at a very crucial juncture in its history, but he gave the choir stalls excellent

39

new backs and pillars of exquisite design and workmanship, as well as hiding the rafters of the church roof with an elaborate moulded plaster ceiling (of the type still to be seen at Levens Hall) which, rightly or wrongly, the Victorians found it necessary to remove but of which pictures happily remain.

Clerical Staff

LITTLE EVIDENCE HAS so far been revealed regarding the numbers and names of the clergy who served the parish of Cartmel in the century which followed the Dissolution of the priory. As we have seen, in 1519 the staff numbered no less than ten, though few precisions regarding their posts are available. The parish priest of Cartmel in 1536 was Oliver Levyns who had a life appointment[132] and a stipend of £6.13s.4d.: a deed of 1607 refers to "Sir Olyvers howses"[133] which were almost certainly the two semi-detached ones at the north east corner of Barngarth, and which he may have purchased, though this is not certain. Brian Willan, a canon of the late priory, was Oliver's successor, as we have seen; he may have lived to be almost 90 (his age was given as 28 in 1536). Unhappily, so far there is no evidence regarding the names and numbers of the secular clergy holding minor posts in the very sizeable parish of Cartmel, though it is known that there were seven of them in 1548.[134] These were reduced to four by 1554 and probably only two by 1562,[135] – probably serving the chapels at Flookburgh and Cartmel Fell, the chantry chapels having all disappeared.

A large part of the priory's modest wealth came from its possession of Cartmel's rectory (a term which did not in those days designate a building inhabited by the incumbent of the parish, but the extensive income legally due from the parishioners of which tithes or tenth parts of produce was much the major item). At the Dissolution this very valuable financial asset became Crown property and thereafter had a very complicated history as the Holker Hall deeds show. It passed through a number of hands, finally becoming part of the possessions of the owners of Holker Hall, who hold a considerable part of the lands formerly owned by the priory. The holders were under a legal obligation to provide spiritual ministrations for the parishioners, but evidently did so on a very ungenerous scale. From this angle the suppression of the priory was a grave spiritual setback. A lease of the rectory to George Preston (the owner of the Holker Hall estates) stated only that he should provide "one or more" sufficient ministers for the widespread but unplutocratic area. Only in Victorian times did it acquire an adequate number of parish clergy.[136]

Part Two

*   *   *

The Buildings

THE CHURCH

The Chronology of the Church's Architecture

A VERY CONSIDERABLE destruction of contemporary documents concerning the history of the priory is particularly marked in the sphere of its architectural development. We now have available only a very small number of early references, all of which are minute. Because of this our knowledge of the history of the conventual buildings, apart from the gatehouse, is virtually a complete blank. So far as the conventual church is concerned, the fact that it is still virtually intact makes it feasible to date its evolution at least approximately, with the aid of certain known dates of allied aspects of its history. It is quite clear that its architecture belongs to three periods. (see Plan).

Period I – (c.1190-c.1220)

To this first period belong (a) the main south door (formerly, perhaps, the cloister door) with a little adjacent walling; (b) the south transept, apart from the two large windows in its south wall and the small blocked window in its east wall; (c) most of the chancel with its magnificent arcades, and the triforium, but not its east window or the clerestory; (d) the north choir aisle or Piper Choir, apart from the two windows in its north wall; (e) the arches of the crossing, despite some slight re-adjustment; (f) the early Gothic door in the north wall of the nave and possibly a small part of the adjacent walling.

    The stylistic features of this first period are of considerable interest, displaying clearly a very intricate mixture of late Romanesque and early Gothic features, which led Pevsner to write "for the architectural

41

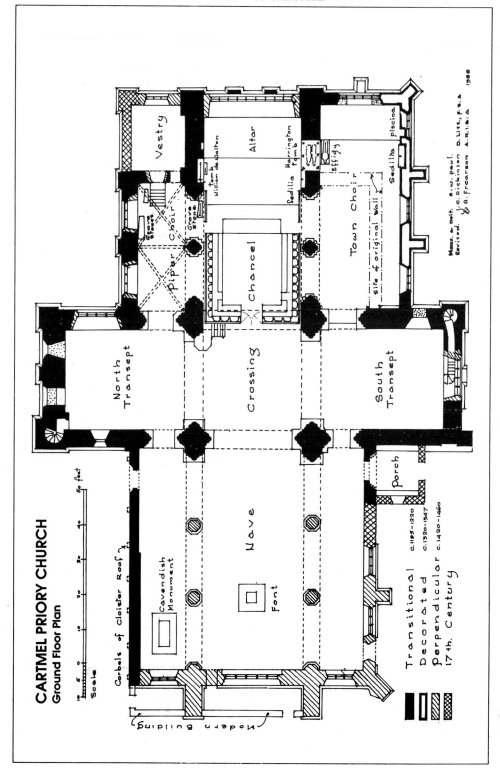

CARTMEL PRIORY CHURCH
Ground Floor Plan

Scale

Corbels of Cloister Roof

Modern Building

Cavendish Monument

Nave

Font

Porch

North Transept

Crossing

South Transept

Piper Choir

Chancel

Town Choir

Grave Stones

Grave Stone

Vestry

tomb William de Walton

Altar

Sedilia

Harrington tomb

Sedilia

Effigy

site of original Wall

Sedilia

Piscina

Transitional c.1195-1220
Decorated c.1320-1347
Perpendicular c.1420-1460
17th. Century

Meas. & Delt. R.W. Paul.
Revised J.C. Dickinson D.Litt., F.S.A
& R. Frearson A.R.I.B.A
1966

historian...Cartmel is of special importance because it can teach what forms were used c.1190 and in the following twenty or thirty years." With what degree of precision can we date this work? As has been seen, the origins of the monastery belong to 1190 or very near that year and work on the new church no doubt began without much delay. All the walling of this period is excellent ashlar and it was intended that both nave and chancel should have twin aisles. This was a luxury by no means found in all comparable houses of Austin canons, but was probably desired by Cartmel's well-endowed and pious founder, William Marshall. However, he died in 1219 and almost certainly his death left the priory with mediocre resources and an unfinished church, so that its building programme was quickly and drastically reduced in scope; at this juncture, possibly but not certainly, the chancel, crossing and transepts of the church were complete, but very little of the nave had been constructed. As Petit pointed out in his very perceptive article on the church published long ago,[137] there are some interesting signs of economy – the arches of both the north and south arcades of the chancel have their outer orders carved only with simple chamfers, in sharp contrast to the luxuriant mouldings on their inner faces. Similarly the arches leading into the north and south aisles of the eastern limb have plain chamfered faces on the eastern sides but richly carved ones on the western ones, whilst the arches at the east end of the nave aisles have their ornate faces on the east and not the west as one might have expected – a rather curious fact which, as Petit plausibly urged, suggests that the nave itself at this time was very short. As he shrewdly comments "the capricious employment of the round and pointed arch is one of the remarkable features of this church" and also points out that it is doubtful "whether a fully developed nave ever existed or was even designed."

Period II – (c.1320 – c.1350)

The work of this period consists solely of the Town Choir or south choir aisle. The Town Choir is termed "Lord Harrington's Quire", in the *Old Church Book* in 1674,[138] and there is little doubt that it was built by Lord John Harrington, (d.1347) to enlarge the old south choir aisle so as to provide more space for the parishioners' worship as well as a place for the elaborate chantry tomb for himself and his wife, which stood in the centre of the western bay of this chapel. We have no precise evidence regarding the chronology of the enterprise, which certainly took a good twenty years to carry through, but various details of the chapel suggest that it was probably largely constructed in the course of the second quarter of the fourteenth century, (the glass of the east window of the chapel is York work and belongs approximately to the period 1320-30).

43

Period III – (c.1420 – c.1460)

This period saw very extensive changes in the buildings of the priory. Unfortunately little documentation concerning them has survived, though at the very end of the 14th century a surviving deed alleges that the priory buildings were then in ruin. Of the various architectural changes which took place, much the most important was the rebuilding of the cloister garth and its attendant buildings on the opposite (northern) side of the nave; a scheme which is probably without parallel in the history of English monastic construction. About the same time almost all of the main original thirteenth century windows of the church were replaced by the much larger ones then in vogue. Perhaps as an economy measure, no largish clerestory windows were inserted, though a completely new nave of a rather cheap construction was built. The only sign of grandeur in this entire programme was the insertion of the magnificent east window, which was almost certainly a benefaction of the great Harrington family, to whom the church was already indebted. One very unusual change was the remodelling of the crossing which produced the striking diagonal belfry tower, giving the priory exterior such a unique look. Of the rebuilt cloister buildings next to no vestige remains, and we have no precise knowledge regarding the alterations made in the church, though the new east window almost certainly belongs to the third decade of the fourteenth century, whilst the misericords have been ascribed to about 1440 or a little earlier.

It is to be noted that the *Old Church Book*[139] (which begins in 1597) shows us that the eastern parts of the priory church formerly bore names some of which are not in use today. The north choir aisle, today called the Piper Choir, is so termed in 1615[140] but almost certainly is also "the Organ Queare" mentioned in 1674.[141] The chancel is termed "that quiere adjoining to the Pyper Choire" in 1615,[142] but in 1618, "the ladie's quiere",[143] and in 1645, "the chancell",[144] the term that is employed today. In 1615 we have mention of "the parish quiere",[145] and in 1618 a new roof was ordered for "the sowthe roufe over the Parish Quiere",[146] but this is a somewhat ambiguous phrase. In 1624 comes a more explicit entry. It was ordered that a clock "shall bee sett in the southe part of the churche called the Paishe Quiere and two dyalls to be made to it, the one thereof to be within the churche and th'other without the churche, out at the windowe over the Old Porche".[147] The first of these ordinances might seem to suggest that the "Parishe Quiere" is what we would term the Town Choir, but the later one makes it quite certain that "the Parish Quiere" included the south transept which is adjoined by the old porch of the Church and still has in its west wall the blocked square hole formerly occupied by the clock here mentioned. In 1674 what is now termed "the Town Choir" is termed "Lord Harrington's Queare".[148] How long this latter very suitable title was in use it is quite impossible to say.

The Chancel

THE ORIGINAL CHANCEL of the monastic church has altered little, except for extensive changes in its fenestration. Although the point is not quite certain, it is probable that the parish church which the first Austin canons found at Cartmel was a smallish building which stood on the site of the northern side of the present south transept and the western part of the area now occupied by the Town Choir. This structure probably continued in use until the western part of the present adjoining chancel was built, but was destroyed when construction of the south choir aisle and south transept had proceeded far enough to make this desirable. This new choir, built adjoining the north side of the old church, was intended for the convent and not for the parishioners. During its building a temporary east wall to the chancel probably was constructed, just east of the great twin arcades arches, its position being indicated by the spot on the south side of the north wall where the dripstone ends. On either side of this choir were built, somewhat later, side-chapels of two bays with simple quadripartite ribbed vaults; the northern of these two chapels remains largely unaltered. The main entrances to these are on the western side and have pointed arches of early Gothic appearance, but the mouldings have a Romanesque look. As is already noted, the mouldings on all the outer sides of these choir arches have nothing more than mere chamfers – perhaps an economy measure.

All the walling of the chancel's north choir aisle and transepts is built from fine squared blocks of ashlar, the internal faces being made from a magnificent lemon-coloured stone which glows gloriously in the sunlight. The external faces of these walls are made of a greyer stone which, as the masons seem to have discovered with great rapidity, resisted weathering far better than that used on the interior. Right round the interior of the walls of the chancel above the arches ran originally a triforium, of which the northern and southern ranges, but not the eastern one, survive intact. The area behind their arcades is very slim indeed. The arches of the triforium are small and of very simple design and workmanship, their little columns having simple rounded capitals with square abaci. The rather unusual design of this triforium arcade may be a simplified version of that of Chartres cathedral which belongs to the last decade of the twelfth century, i.e. about the date building at Cartmel had begun, and is very similar. The founder of the priory had various French connections.

The clerestory windows of the nave are simple and spare – only two in each wall consisting of twin lights with cusped heads and of very minor size. The clerestory windows of the transepts are very simple, being nothing more than small very slim rectangular windows of one light. Those in the chancel are also small and simple, having two lights with cusped heads; they belong to the time when the chancel was re-furbished in the first half of the fifteenth century as do the curious rectangular recesses which adjoin them. Originally, following what was a stock pattern amongst other houses of Austin canons in this country, the north and south walls of the chancel projected beyond the side aisles and each had a large lancet window which provided invaluable light for the high altar area. At Cartmel, however, in process of time both these lancets went out of use, through extensions of the side aisles of the chancel. As we shall see, that on the south side was lost when the south choir aisle was enlarged, whilst that on the north side disappeared through the addition of a smallish 15th century sacristy, which was much rebuilt and enlarged in the 17th century. In the east wall of the original chancel were two rows of three lancets, superimposed, with the triforium passage running between them, and linking with that in the side walls.

The East Window

IN THE FIRST half of the fifteenth century the priory acquired one of its most magnificent features, when the east wall of the chancel was largely monopolised by a huge and magnificent window, very comparable with that in the mighty minster at York, with which it has connections.

How was it that this noble and very expensive adjunct was set up in a remote and far from affluent priory? To the present writer the answer to

Left:
The East Window

46

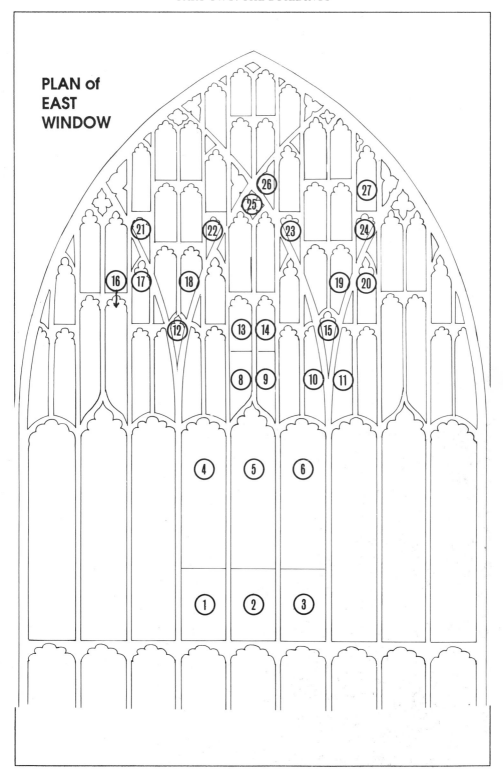

**PLAN of
EAST
WINDOW**

this question seems clear, even if not totally beyond all doubt. The priory itself certainly had not the wealth to pay for it from its own resources nor had the very poor population of the locality. The only well-to-do magnates living in the South Cumbria area were the Harringtons, whose early seat was at Aldingham and who owned Wraysholme, not far from the priory. By the early fourteenth century this family had risen to major importance. The then head was Lord John Harrington, whose summons to Parliament as a peer from 1324 onwards made him the first such dignitary in our area. He died in 1347 and founded in Cartmel priory a chantry wherein he and his wealthy wife Joan were buried, in an elaborate tomb much of which still survives to delight posterity. Although Conishead priory was nearer to the family home at Aldingham than Cartmel and certainly received benefactions from the family, there is no doubt that Cartmel was the family's main monastic love, and there is other evidence which supports very strongly indeed the theory that the great east window here was acquired with Harrington cash.

On 8th June 1417 "John de Haryngton, Knight, Lord of Aldingham" as the document calls him, made his will, therein stating that he was "purposing to visit foreign parts without the kingdom of England".[149] Perhaps because it was made in a hurry, his will was much shorter and less elaborate than was usual for a grandee of his rank. The number of specific bequests is very small, much the most important clause enacting "the residue of all my goods and the debts remaining due to me I will that my executors shall dispose of and distribute in the manner in which for the safety of my soul shall befit them to be done".[150] To any trained medievalist it is obvious that alms to religious bodies, especially to any with which the family of the testator was closely connected, was a *sine qua non* when a will had to be executed. Thus, in view of the very intimate connection of the Harringtons with Cartmel and the fact that the priory's huge east window was certainly begun within a very few years of the death of this Lord John Harrington, it is highly likely that it was a memorial to him. His will was proved on 26th April 1418 and his window may well have been ordered very soon after this. The late Dr Peter Newton, having devoted much study to medieval glass at York, had no doubt that this Cartmel glass was made in that city in the third decade of the century or very near it. Its tracery is now known to be of Tadcaster stone whilst that of the mullions is from Quarry Flat, whence had come so much of the stone of the priory. It has nine lights, grouped in threes, the centre one of each group having an ogee head, the rest being pointed.

The window is crossed by a central transom, below which no old glass now remains. In the area between the transom and the tracery of the head of the window are the three central lights, each of which now contain a large figure. That on the north side is in perfect condition, whilst the adjoining two are somewhat damaged (the southernmost of these three was moved to its present position as part of the very modern restoration, having previously been in the light which adjoins its present southern side). Just below each of these major figures are minor miscellaneous scraps of glass, whilst the tracery above retains a considerable part (though far from all) of its ancient glass *in situ*, as the chart shows.[151]

THE GLASS

I. Fragments: (in the part of the window below the transom).
1. *Northern side* – a head of St. Peter; the head and shoulders of an archbishop saint; the head of a male saint; a large composite figure of an archbishop saint blessing and a few fragments of inscriptions.

4. St William of York   **5. Our Lady and the Holy Child**

2. *Central light* – a hand with a cup, perhaps from an Adoration of the Magi scene; the head of an angel; eagles standing in foliage; fragment of a Nine Orders of Angels panel; a complete representation of St. Peter, shown enthroned and vested as Pope with the triple papal mitre, blessing with a church held in his left hand.

3. *Southern side* – fragment, probably of a virgin martyr; female saint wearing a fillet studded with roses; head of an angel; a large figure of Christ enthroned with his right hand in blessing and an orb in his left hand; small fragments of inscriptions.

II. Full Size Figures: (in the area above the transom).

4. *An Archbishop Saint* – (undamaged) – probably but not certainly St. William of York. He is shown nimbed, his right hand is raised in blessing, his left hand holds an archi-episcopal cross. He wears mass vestments, over which is a pallium. Above is an architectural canopy with a half length frontal angel in its centre, as in the adjoining two lights (the two outer backgrounds are red, the centre one blue).

5. *Our Lady and the Holy Child* – (somewhat damaged; – She is shown seated, suckling the Holy Child (whose head is missing). She is crowned and holds a sceptre in her right hand; her robes are rich, with jewelled hems.

6. *St. John the Baptist* – shown seated in a book with the Agnus Dei in his right hand, a blue background; the lower part and canopy are incomplete.

7. *Tracery above no. 4*

Left:
6. St. John The Baptist

50

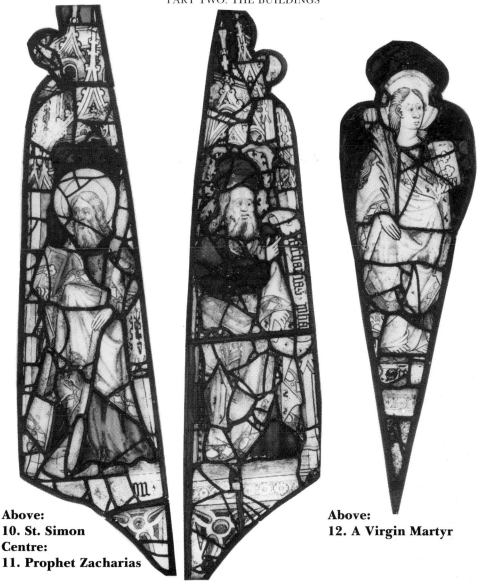

Above:
10. St. Simon
Centre:
11. Prophet Zacharias

Above:
12. A Virgin Martyr

III.   The Tracery Lights: (in the head of the window).

8.   *St. Bartholomew* – (in excellent condition; – his left hand points to a large knife in his right hand, below is inscribed *Bartholome(us)*.

9.   *St. Matthew* – a halberd in his right hand, in his left a scroll inscribed *Scs Matheu*.

10. *St. Simon* – holds a book in his right hand and a large oar in his left – incomplete label.

11. *The Prophet Zacharias* – in his right hand a scroll inscribed *Zacharias propheta*.

12. *A Female Saint* – holding a book in her left hand and a martyr's palm in her right.

51

Left: 27. Archbishop Saint
Centre: 15. A Bishop Saint
Right: 19. St Leonard

13. *Angel Evangelist* – (with the symbol of St. Matthew) and an incomplete scroll *Scs M......*
14. *St. Andrew* – he holds in his right hand a large saltire cross in front of him, in his left hand, a scroll inscribed *Scs Andreas.*
15. *A Bishop Saint* – (composite).
16. *An angel* – (incomplete) holding a scroll? inscribed *Scs Matthew.*
17. *Prophet Ezekiel (?)* – Composite.
18. *St. Agnes* – has the right hand raised and the left hand missing.
19. *St. Leonard* – wears mass vestments and holds a book in his right hand, a crozier in his left; below on a label *Scs Leonardus.*

Left: 20. Prophet Isaiah
Centre: 21. A Female Martyr
Right: 22. A Female Saint

20. *Prophet Isaiah* – he points to a scroll in his left hand labelled *Ysaias propheta.*
21. *Female Saint* – crowned, holds a book in her left hand and a martyr's palm in her right.
22. *A Female Saint.*
23. *A non-descript composite figure.*
24. *A Bishop Saint* – he wears mass vestments and holds a crozier in his left hand.
25. *Head of God the Father (in situ)* – frontal with an elaborate nimbus.
26. *An Angel* – right hand raised, a palm in the left hand inscribed *angelus.*
27. *An Archbishop Saint.*

(Some unidentified "old glass" is known to have been lost in the early 19th century).

An old book of antiquarian notes written by one Gibson of Bowness (the present whereabouts of which is unknown), quoted by the indispensable Stockdale, shows us that there were then in this window no less than three coats of arms of the Harrington family and one each of the de Roos of Kendal, the Stricklands of Sizergh and the Redmans of Levens, as well as the post-medieval arms of the Prestons of Holker.[152]

Here we may note that although there is little other medieval glass remaining in the priory, some very interesting glass which was originally here, is preserved elsewhere in the neighbourhood, at St. Martin's parish church of Bowness. This church was much damaged by a fire in 1487 and soon after acquired a fine new east window which is largely fitted with pre-Reformation glass. The main part of this was originally made for it – a large crucifixion scene, and the statues of St. George, St. Katherine and St. Barbara. To the same period belongs the very fine coat of arms of a Prince-of-Wales above it, which probably pertained to King Henry VII's son Arthur (1486-1502) – whose very unexpected presence here may have some connection with the fact that Christopher Bainbridge, the Archbishop of York from 1508-1514 and who was Cumbrian born, was confessor to Prince Arthur's parents.

In the head of the window is a good deal of glass mostly heraldic, arranged in very higgledy-piggledy fashion, which almost certainly came largely or wholly from Cartmel priory and was probably bought (very cheaply) at the time of the dissolution of the monastery. Most of the

**Glass in
St. Martin's Parish
Church, Bowness**

**Donor panel –
St. Martin's Parish
Church, Bowness**

heraldic glass seems largely to belong to the first half of the fifteenth century, when, as we have seen, an extensive restoration of the priory was under way and pertains to local families. Very significantly, it includes the coat of Lord Grey of Ruthen (d.1440) who had inherited the position of patron of Cartmel priory and as such would certainly have contributed towards its major restoration.[153]

Also to be seen is a little non-heraldic glass (probably also from Cartmel) including an attractive and early panel showing Our Lady, whilst at the bottom of this Bowness window are two specially interesting and unusual panels with a Cartmel connection. That in the northernmost light shows a kneeling tonsured figure in monastic garb from whose mouth issues an invaluable label which was formerly inscribed *William Plo......prior of Cartmel.* This lettering is no longer visible and the name has been wrongly read as John. In the next light but one is shown a group of five figures similarly garbed each having a similar label bearing his name:– these titles are known to have been Thomas Hogson, Willym Bareaye, Will (Purfoot), Roger Thwaytts and George Fish(wick) – all but the third being common local names.[154]

The sanctuary area adjoining the great east window of Cartmel priory church has undergone no few changes, including an extensive 17th century refit, still to be glimpsed in one or two old prints but largely obliterated by one of those very radical overhauls to which our Victorian forebears were so grossly addicted. Of the latter, major relics now visible are the elaborately tiled floor so typical of the epoch, and the massive

Belgian oak chairs presented to the church by the 7th Duke of Devonshire, one of which has a label inscribed *Adèle d'Henin*. The present altar and its ornaments, with the prayer desk, were put in some fifty years ago. The Victorians had placed here a reredos with somewhat horrific paintings of the apostles which disappeared at the same time.

Notable among the medieval relics in the sanctuary is the large tombstone under the low arch in the north wall. Made from polished local limestone it bears the neatly cut marginal inscription HIC JACET WILELMUS DE WALTONA – "Here lies William of Walton prior of Cartmel" – (the Walton here mentioned is a mile from the village and is mentioned in Domesday Book, but is now only a farm). The tombstone has two unusual features. Firstly the brevity of the inscription. One might have expected there would have been added to it *cuius anima propicietur Deus* ("on whose soul may God have mercy") along with the date of William's death; the fact that the tombstone is a long one with a very short inscription caused the letters of the latter to be set unusually far apart. Secondly, the letters of the inscription are cut much deeper and more elaborately than usual. Recent research by Dr J. Blair[155] has shown that there must have been inserted in them originally grand brass letters of a type which had just become commercialised in England at the time of Prior William de Walton; he is known to have been prior of Cartmel in the last years of the thirteenth century and possibly a little later, though the precise dates of his priorate are uncertain. In a letter to the author, Dr Blair writes of this slab, "It is odd to find such a high-quality product in a part of the country which otherwise had virtually no early brasses at all. The design is clearly influenced by London patterns...The date should be somewhere in the range c.1300-40." As prior William was evidently alive in 1299 but probably died fairly soon after, the stone may be almost as early as the earliest of the London prototypes which it copies. Up-to-date knowledge at a place so remote as Cartmel, may have been acquired by the prior when he went off to the big outside world to attend a general chapter of his Order or some such assembly, or it may have been presented by one of the wealthy Harringtons.

In the pavement near this tomb is a small uninscribed slab with a floriated cross about which nothing is known. Just east of the Walton tomb is a small blocked door constructed in the fifteenth century when a small low sacristy was added to the north choir aisle; the floor level here was quite unreasonably raised in 1864. In pre-Victorian times there was also in the floor of the sanctuary a slab inscribed HIC JACET WILLS. BR......QUONDAM P'OR, the present whereabouts of which is unknown; this may well commemorate the canon who was prior for all or most of the time when the re-building was under way.

At the northern end of the east wall of the sanctuary can be seen remains of a small aumbry or cupboard, blocked up by the Victorians.

The Choir Stalls

High up in the south east corner of the sanctuary is a small stone ledge, possible meant to hold a light. The south wall of the sanctuary is dominated by the massive Harrington tomb, whose (post-Reformation) insertion largely obliterated the original lancet window here and grievously damaged the elegant mid-thirteenth century sedilia further west. Adjoining the eastern side of the Harrington tomb, low down in the wall, are the very slight remains of a small piscina of Transitional date.

The Choir Stalls

AS WE HAVE SEEN, manufacture of the seats and benches of the choir stalls has been assigned to about 1430-40[156] and that of the attendant screens and canopies to the early 17th century. All of the misericords but one have survived. They are vigorously carved and so excellently preserved as to suggest that they were carefully protected at and after the Dissolution when the roof above them almost certainly suffered some damage. Their carved faces all have small carvings flanking them, most of which show foliage of various types, though there are a number of heads of beasts real or imaginary, and a few miscellaneous subjects.

South Side

1.   (The prior's seat) – *Arabesque*, (Capital letters W, for the William who was prior of Cartmel at the time of manufacture).

2. *A crowned head with three noses and three mouths with foliage –*
    representing that of one of the *macrobii,* a mythical race thought to
    live in India; used here to symbolise the Trinity; (both foliage).

3. *A pelican feeding her young with flesh from her breast,* symbolising
    Christ who gave up His life for men; (foliage; a head).

4. *A half-length figure of an angel* holding a blank shield; (fruit; foliage).

5. *An ape holding a flask,* being a satire on doctors who were held to be untrustworthy as monkeys; (a bird with fruit; foliage).

6. *A double-tailed mermaid with a comb in one hand, and a mirror in the other*; symbolising the lusts of the flesh; (a fish representing the Christian soul fleeing from the mermaid; foliage).

7. *A crowned figure seated in a very large basket to which two large birds are fastened* – a pictorial representation of the medieval legend of "Alexander's Flight". This relates that the emperor of this name sought to find the edge of the world (which was thought to be flat and circular and not spherical). Having arrived at what he thought to be his destination, he decided to check on this by becoming airborne in the large basket with its attendant birds which he tempted to go upwards by dangling a piece of meat on a spear just above their heads. Having as he thought achieved his desire, he manoeuvred them back to earth by use of the same stratagem, landing a very long

61

way from his base; (A letter T with a leaf and foliage; in the elbow of the stall near the letter is a very curious little carving of a dragon (?) caught in a trap, and twisted into the form of a letter T).

8.   *A dragon with flapping wings*; (a flower (?) with a human face in its centre; foliage).

9.   *A peacock with outspread tail* – the emblem of immortality; (foliage; a bat with a human face, hanging upside down).

Above:
Bowness Church - East Window

Right:
Bowness Church - Canons of Cartmel

Left:
Cartmel Priory
East Window

i) a composite angel
ii) St. Andrew
iii) Bishop Saint
iv) St. Matthew

10. *An eagle (?) in flight with a bunch of grapes in its beak*; (foliage).

11. *Two large birds feeding from a sack or bowl of corn* – (fruit and flowers).

12. *A grinning foliate face*; (foliage; foliage).

13. *Intricate design of serrated leaves* (?); (fruit with leaves;? rose and leaves).

North Side, from the west

14. *An oak tree, in the trunk of which a unicorn is caught by its horn.*
Medieval lore taught that the best way of capturing a unicorn was to
get it to charge into a tree embedding its horn therein, – the animal
was thus the "type" of Adam who also 'fell through a tree'; (foliage;
foliage).

15. *Stiff leaf foliage;* (foliage; mask).

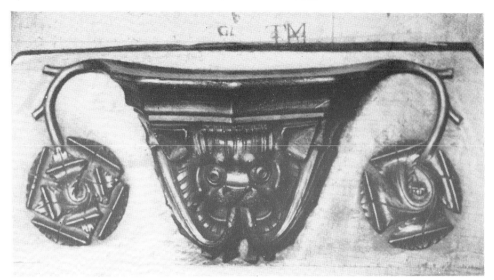

16. *Mask of a grinning lion with foliage (?) issuing from its mouth;* (foliage; foliage).

17. Lost.

18. *A griffin;* (animal mask; animal mask).

19. *Man's head with curly hair, beard, whiskers and ornamental hat; (a leaf; a mask).*

20. *A large double rose between leaves; (head of an ox; fruit and leaves).*

21. *A deer chased by three dogs*; (a crowned letter W with a small heart and flower on the label attached on both sides; a hedgehog).

22. *Three intertwined acanthus leaves*; (flower; mask).

23. *An elephant with a howdah, leaning against a tree.* Contemporaries thought that an elephant's legs had no joints so the beast could be captured by getting it to lean against a tree whose trunk had been largely sawn through so that the beast crashed under its weight – this being a reminder of Adam who also "fell through a tree"; (flowers and leaves, lion mask).

24. *An elaborate bunch of pendant leaves*; (foliage; foliage).

25. *A winged and clawed demon or dragon*; (rosette; mask).

26. *A spray of two large leaves* – (foliage; foliage).

The designs of the misericords on the northern stalls are mostly much simpler with more subjects taken from nature than those on the south side, so may be the work of a different carver.

The upper parts of the stalls with their elegant Corinthian columns and elaborate pierced screens are one of the most striking manifestations of the generosity of George Preston (d.1640), one of the greatest benefactors that the church of Cartmel has had since it was founded. His family, like many northern gentry in his time were conservative in religion. The elder branch of the family acquired Furness Abbey and much of its property at the Dissolution. George was a junior member of the family, and in 1610 bought the manor of Cartmel along with the site of the priory and various other adjuncts, for the then very sizeable sum of £2,200. Very quickly, as the precise details preserved in the *Old Church Book* show us, he initiated a massive overhaul of the fabric and fittings of the priory. As his curious epitaph on the painted memorial to his family now on the north wall of the nave records, "the said George out of his zeal to God at his great charge repaired this Church being in great decay with a new roofe of timber and beautified it within very decently with fresh plaister work and adorned the chancel with curious carved woodwork and placed therein a paire or organs of great value."

The screens and pillars of his choir stalls are very liberally carved with a large array of the instruments of the Passion Of Christ, and are of truly first class workmanship. Whether the old tradition that they were made by Flemish craftsmen is correct or not is uncertain. It should be noted that the screens are very extensively pierced, so would not provide that considerable protection against draughts and cold which had been a main motive for their existence in medieval days. (When the flooring of some of the choir stalls was removed a fair amount of remains of bracken was found beneath – was this a primitive form of hassock?).

It is likely that in pre-Reformation times the organ sat on the west side of the choir screen, over the main entrance to the chancel. But Mr Preston probably moved it to the west end of the Piper Choir where the uncarved nature of part of the screenwork suggests that it was placed – (as we have noted, the Piper Choir was also termed "the Organ Quire"). This organ was certainly smashed up by the inhibited Cromwellians, as a sad note in the *Old Church Book* of 28th November 1643 confirms, soon after their visit – "there was left furthe of the vestrie xiii peeces of the sides and leaves of the organ and the winde cheste, also a peece of old aldmerie and iij peeces more of wood set with organ sides".[157] After this at an uncertain date, the new organ was placed on the screen, above the main (western) entrance to the choir.

The Town Choir (The South Choir Aisle or Harrington Choir)

THE FIRST MAJOR alteration to the original structure of Cartmel priory church was the re-building of the south choir aisle on a very much larger scale, the new internal dimensions being 94ft long by 58ft broad, as against 34ft long by 15ft broad originally. The simple lancet windows were replaced by four of the broad elaborate traceried windows then in fashion, the three of them on the south side being separated by the deep buttresses by now in vogue. Perhaps for warmth and to avoid expense, the old vaulted roof was replaced by a flat wooden ceiling; the three corbels

71

The Town Choir

which supported it remain, including one showing Samson wrestling with the lion.

Two unusual features mark this new building. Firstly, either from love of uniformity or to save expense or both, most and perhaps all of the fine old ashlar with its drip moulding was retained, and was probably augmented by materials to match it from the same quarry as the old one. Secondly, the easternmost and westernmost windows of the new south wall have tracery which instead of being similar to that of the centre one have patterns which are certainly very much earlier. In his useful handbook on Decorated windows Sharpe comments that these two are "of considerable interest...of very early date. Their form is somewhat uncommon, for although they contain the usual geometrical figures, their arrangement is peculiar...". Of one of them he notes "the singular design of the central figure, which contains a species of very uncommon cusp".[158] We have no documentary evidence regarding the date of these two, but they can scarcely be later than 1330 and may be appreciably earlier. By contrast, the middle window in the south wall of the choir and that in its eastern wall have flowing tracery that must belong to the middle of the century or thereabouts. This suggests that the re-building of the south choir aisle was carried out in two stages. First a gap was made

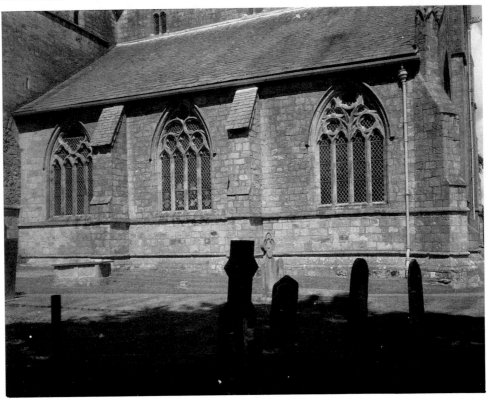

The South Wall of the Town Choir

between the east and west ends of the old south wall with their windows by demolishing the centre walling and another gap created by pulling down the east wall of the original choir aisle. This work would have a double use. It would facilitate the removal of extensive débris of the old aisle, notably of its ponderous ribbed vault, and would also allow easy movement for the transport of the extensive timbers prepared for the new roof. In the fragmentary ends of the south wall, new windows were inserted. There probably followed a pause in construction for one or two decades, suggested as very likely by the tracery of the windows and may well have been due to the immense damage wrought by the Scots in the north of England in the years after the great Scottish raids of 1316 and 1322 which put large areas out of cultivation and made it necessary to make very considerable reductions in the taxable value of benefices. (In the diocese and arch-deaconry to which Cartmel priory was situate, the valuation of the churches of Aldingham, Cartmel and Ulverston were reduced by over eighty per cent and that of their temporal possessions by even more). The new walls and roof of the chapel were probably not completed for some twenty years later than the early parts. Almost certainly this re-building of the south choir aisle together with the creation therein of a chantry for himself and his wife was the brain-child of Lord John Harrington, who may well have paid all or most of the costs himself.

Until the Victorians and their very recent successors monstrously disfigured it by housing in it the priory organ, the Town Choir was a place of great beauty and great practicality. Its comparatively low roof and its few and smallish arches made it far less frigid than most parts of the church, whilst its position on the south side of the chancel allowed its spacious windows to let in a maximum amount of sun in that early part of the day in which the major part of medieval services were held. The modest amount of the original glass preserved is of high quality York work, dated about 1320-40. Most of it is in the east window where the main lights retain only three panels of a complex "Rod of Jessee", illustrating what were believed to be the earthly ancestors of Christ. Jesse was originally portrayed here at the bottom of a tree whence branches arose showing his descendants above him. In the head of the east window were two small panels showing the Angel announcing to Our Lady that she should be the earthly mother of Christ. Of these the figure of the latter has been destroyed, but the former is intact and is of singular beauty – (it was displayed in a comparatively recent exhibition of 14th century art at the Louvre).

After the Reformation the eastern end of this chapel was appropriated as the private chapel of the Prestons and Lowthers who successively acquired the Holker Hall estate (which included a large portion of the former possessions of Cartmel priory). Several ostentatious memorials of

**Town Choir
East Window –
Fragments of
Rod of Jesse**

the 17th and 18th centuries commemorate them. Towards the east end of the south wall is a small sedilia of only two seats instead of the usual three; its arches have ogee heads made partly of red sandstone, partly of the yellow used in almost all the rest of the church. The size of this chapel and the presence of the sedilia shows clearly enough that when it was built it was intended for public worship and not merely for private masses, a feature almost certainly dictated by the fact that at the time of its erection the priory still lacked a reasonably large nave – (as we have seen, by what was also a very unusual arrangement indeed, at Cartmel the parishioners also used for their worship the south transept).

On the north side of the chapel stands the old font, made in the early thirteenth century; its bowl has been grievously hacked about (perhaps by the Victorians). As the picture of it in Dugdale's *Monasticon* makes abundantly clear it was originally surmounted by a curious pyramidical font cover, dated 1640. This old font was replaced by a Victorian effusion (now at the west end of the nave) and was then sent to Flookburgh, but has returned to Cartmel comparatively recently. Two attractive housel benches of the 17th century replace the usual altar rails. In the west face of the main pier is a shallow niche for a statue. This chapel, being probably the legal successor of the little parish church which preceded the priory, would have been dedicated to St. Michael.

The Harrington Tomb

INSERTED IN THE north wall of this chapel are the battered but considerable remains of the so-called "Harrington tomb", "one of the best of its date in England", as Pevsner has recently claimed. It is one of the very limited number commemorating top-ranking medieval aristocrats of which substantial remains have survived in northern England. Properly speaking, it is not a tomb, but the battered remains of a chantry chapel, founded in memory of Lord John Harrington (d.1347) and his wife Joan (née Dacre) both of whose family arms were formerly very visible on the monument. Almost certainly this chantry chapel was originally situated in the centre of the western bay of the Town Choir, where signs of it were seen when the area now engrossed by the organ was recently temporarily opened up. Originally the chantry must have been of two small bays, with a stone altar at its eastern end. Almost certainly this altar was destroyed and the rest of the tomb badly damaged by Cromwellian soldiers who spent the night of 1st October 1643 at Cartmel after a minor battle in Furness. Although it is quite clear that in their stay they displayed that fanatical iconoclasm for which they were notorious, doubtless because of the briefness of their sojourn, very considerable remains of the Harrington tomb have nevertheless survived.

Probably very soon after its maltreatment, it was decided by the then

The Harrington Tomb (south side)

owner of Holker, Mr Thomas Preston, a very pious "church papist", to reconstruct elsewhere the sadly battered remains of the chantry. The safest place for them was wisely thought to be at the east end of the wall which divides the sanctuary from the Town Choir. Such a position meant that one side of the tomb was adjacent to the sanctuary, the other being part of the north wall of the Town Choir, the eastern end of which at an uncertain date after the Dissolution became the private chapel of the highly conservative owners of Holker Hall. The choice of this position for the vandalised monument probably explains why the sculpture on the south side of the tomb is much less damaged than that on the other. Much, but by no means all of the original structure of the chantry was roughly fitted in here, and still remains. Its insertion entailed the destruction of part of the main sedilia and of a large recess in the south side of the wall which probably contained the fine effigy of a prior of the house, which was then moved on to the floor below where it still remains.

Originally, as was usual in such cases, the Harrington tomb was brightly painted, but at an unknown date – perhaps in the 18th century – most of the remaining decoration was covered with whitewash, which was later removed much too vigorously by the Victorians. As a result the only remains of the original medieval painting which has survived is that on most (though not all) of the under side of the tester or canopy which is set on high over the effigies.

The tomb[159] consists of the four main elements:–

1. *The great stone chest.* This originally contained the mortal remains of Lord John Harrington and his wife Joan (née Dacre) and is 6ft long, 5ft 6ins broad and 3ft 3ins high. Its sides are skilfully carved with an elaborate diamond diaper pattern, which on the south side incorporates the escallop or shell which dominated the Dacre coat of arms.

   At the bases of each corner of the chest were carved the traditional symbols of the Four Evangelists – on the south side are the ox of St. Luke and the eagle of St. John, both fairly well preserved; on the north are what are evidently the damaged man of Matthew and the almost totally destroyed lion of St. Mark. Between them are carved a series of small seated figures in monastic costume engaged in singing what is presumably a requiem. The precentor is shown beating time with uplifted hand and one group of three canons share a large service book sustained by a lectern, (this being the maximum number allowed to do this by their observances). Along the north and south sides of the top of the chest is a series of small figures, almost certainly representing Austin canons. Very surprisingly these are cut in the same block of stone as the chest – "this is a unique feature" comments the ultra-learned Pevsner.

In 1835 the chest of the tomb was opened under the leadership of the local antiquary, Mr William Field, with the consent of the then incumbent, the Rev. Thomas Remington. To discover what was found we must rely on the inadequate notes given in Stockdale's *Annals of Cartmel* (1872) "in the midst of the cavity which was of considerable size, there appeared a small heap of bones, both those of the human species and of birds; lime rubbish, pieces of thick leather, rusty iron and some part of a skull containing a number of perfectly sound teeth, all promiscuously mixed together". Also found were a piece of leather stitched doublet, a small round piece of iron about half an inch in diameter, highly oxidised, the thigh bone and leg bone of a large bird and a molar tooth "very sound and perfect".[160] Some of these were then in the possession of Mr James Field of Cartmel, a relative of the late Mr Field, along with the tooth given to him by "the late clerk of Cartmel church", Wm. Fell, who obtained it when the tomb was open. Elsewhere mention is made of other oddments, which may have come from the tomb which included "a large piece of stout leather twelve inches by ten with about half of the left armhole, thought to have been part of a leather doublet" and "several pieces of rusty iron like nails, perhaps coffin nails an inch and a half long".[161] The present writer's grandmother, Lucy Agnes Butterworth (née Remington), informed him that as a small child when staying at Aynsome – the family residence – she remembers being told that bones from the Harrington tomb were stored in a tin in a chest-of-drawers there, but she was too frightened to explore further! The Remingtons sold up Aynsome and its contents some sixty years ago, when these relics may well have disappeared, after having, of course, been originally acquired by the Rev. Thomas Remington. Some of the other finds are now displayed in a case in the south transept, and are of very minor interest.

2. *The effigies.* On the top of the tomb chest lie the effigy of Lord John Harrington (exactly six feet long) with that of his wife on his right-hand side which is five feet six inches long. The latter is very little damaged, but there is a large ugly crack across the face of Joan's husband and a little damage to his armour. The heads of them both are each supported by a pair of angels which, like the statuettes of canons which process around the effigies, have been mutilated. Both figures are shown with their hands uplifted and holding a conical object representing a heart, perhaps in memory of the injunction in the Mass "Lift up year hearts". Lord John's feet rest on a lion, perhaps since knights should emulate its bravery, those of his wife on a somewhat damaged dog whose fidelity she should emulate. Lady Joan wears a very loose-fitting dress stretching down to her feet

The Harrington Tomb – Effigies of Lord John Harrington and his wife

whose folds are contained at the waist by a broadish belt, and a veil and wimple. Her husband wears the type of helmet known as a basnet and full chain armour, together with a surcoat that, like the shield on his left hand side bears the *fretty* coat of arms of his family. His sword hangs from a heavy belt, his right leg is crossed over the left leg at its calf. There are signs of grills having protected the outer side of the tomb on top of which the effigies rest. Recent examination has shown that the stone from which the effigies are made is almost certainly local, but the standard of carving is so very much higher than the rest of the tomb that it was almost certainly the work of an outside craftsman. A rough sketch of part of the tomb made by Dodsworth has been published[162] and shows what is apparently boarding behind the heads of the effigies, painted with the arms of Dacre and Harrington.

3. *Corner Columns and Arches.* At the corner of the chest are stout columns which support the ceiling of the tomb, between which on their north and south sides rise elegant ogee arches which support the tomb tester or ceiling. The heads of both these arches have carved thereon a representation of a soul being drawn up to heaven in a sheet by a pair of angels. The arches are each sub-divided by much damaged tracery which rises from a short central pillar. That on the south side has modern work along with medieval work. The small central pillar on the north side is intact and shows a seated figure (? Christ) blessing. Above are three shields, the top one of which displays the *fretty* coat of Harrington, below which is one of the Dacre family.

The corner columns have triple bands of sculpture:

a). *Bottom – small statues of the saints*

S.W. – St. Peter with his key; Our Lady with the Holy Child; St. Michael with a very large trumpet.

S.E. – St. Katherine with her wheel; an empty niche; St. Michael as before.

N.E. – An unidentifiable figure; St. John the Baptist with his *Agnus Dei* emblem; above a censing angel.

N.W. – An unidentifiable figure; an archbishop.

81

b). *Top* –   rather poorly carved scenes from the life of Christ.

S.W. – The scourging of Christ, His hands shown bound around a very slim pillar.

S.E. –   The crucified body of Christ.

N.W. – The blindfolded Christ being buffetted.

N.E. – St. Mary Magdalen drying Christ's feet with her hair.

Between these two bands of carving are carved a number of shields.

S.W. – a blank shield.

S.E. –   a tilting shield.

N.W. – two blank shields (? modern copies).

N.E. – two blank shields (? modern copies).

4. *The Ceiling*

The four corner columns of the tomb support a massive stone frame in which was set an elaborate wooden ceiling or tester, whose under side was originally very elaborately painted. Unhappily some timbers which formed the top part of it disappeared long ago and most of the painting which remains is in far from perfect condition. Originally there were in its four corners the symbols of the four evangelists. At the top were those of St. Mark and St. John, which have totally disappeared, but at the bottom of the tester those of St. Matthew ʹand St. Luke (a man and a winged bull) remain in excellent condition and are very skilfully depicted. Just above the latter is a row of four stars in imperfect condition, which were probably originally joined by a similar set below the symbols of the other two evangelists; similar rows run along the borders of the long sides of the tester. The dominating feature of the ceiling is a large central figure of Christ. He is shown seated, with His right hand elevated in blessing and His left holding an orb (the symbol of the world which he ruled). He wears a long scarlet tunic from which His feet protrude, but most of the garment is now missing. Over the tunic was a blue or greenish cloak (now barely visible) secured by a morse and lined with vair. Of His head nothing remains. Until very recently whitewash and dirt obscured much of the above detail and

Right:
Restoration of the tester

Below:
Portion of the tester
before restoration

the remaining boards of the tester were no longer in their right order. Happily in 1985 it was skilfully restored by Miss A. Hulbert, as far as was feasible.

What is the age of the Harrington tomb? It is unfortunate that we cannot give a very precise answer to this question, owing to the inadequacy of surviving documentary evidence. The sole fact of which we can be quite certain is that of Lord John Harrington's death in 1347. But it was quite common for medieval grandees to prepare their tombs before they died, and it is at least feasible that its effigies were made at a different time from the chest and canopy around them. An attempt has been made to date the effigies from the stylistic evidence of the armour. Ward Perkins claimed that the armour of Lord John shown on his effigy is "at least twenty years earlier in date than 1347", and argues that "the body armour and sword belt are of a type that was generally obsolete by c.1325. The effigy must fall between the fifteen years 1310-25".[163] But he also admits that the canopy and its ornament "appears to belong to the second quarter of the 14th century". Crossley dates the monument to c.1340.[164]

Anyone versed in the history of the Lake Counties knows how very unwise it is not to make full allowance for the time-lag which often separates work in it from that in southern England, as is shown, for

Effigy of a Prior

Tombstone of Prior William of Walton

example, by the fact that the Runic alphabet was being used in Furness for some time after it was extinct in most of the rest of the country. To rely heavily on stylistic evidence to date armour with precision is certainly perilous. In a letter to the present writer the Master of the Armouries, Mr A. V. S. Norman points out that parallels to Lord John's mail and helmet have been found in Yorkshire "as late as the 1330s, as have examples of his type of sword belt". In view of this it would be unwise to dogmatise over the precise date of the effigies and the rest of the tomb. As these elements were almost certainly made by different workmen, it is not impossible that they were carved at different times, but both probably belong to the second quarter of the fourteenth century.

On the top of the tomb now, as in Whitaker's day, are several loose bits of carving. Their original habitat is uncertain but some of them, at least, may have been connected with the little altar at the east end of the chantry chapel. Those on the north side may have formed part of a set depicting the Coronation of the Virgin, those on the south side are a miscellany, and possibly not all of one date.

Perhaps about the time at which the Harrington chantry was constructed, an effigy of an Austin canon who was probably the prior of Cartmel at this time, was carved from the same rather distinctive stone as that of the effigies of Lord and Lady Harrington, and placed in a sizeable recess in the north wall of the Town Choir, was largely destroyed when the Harrington tomb was inserted there in the seventeenth century. Only the base of the recess is now visible. Probably at this time also the effigy was placed in its present position on the floor on the south side of the Harrington tomb on a stone base the top of which is, oddly, of red sandstone. The effigy shows the same skilful workmanship as the Harrington effigy and was probably done at the same time by the same carver. Of the very few medieval effigies of Austin canons in England (there are others at Hexham, Eddington and St. Bartholomew's, Smithfield) this is much superior to the first two and vies with the third in quality. The head of the figure is supported by two badly damaged angels and its feet rest on a somewhat complex dragon in poor condition. The prior, if as is likely, such he be, wears what is probably a long cassock over which is a rochet or surplice with very wide open sleeves which is covered by the very long cloak (cappa) to which the usual very capacious hood is attached, and is here shown neatly folded back behind the head, which rests on a small cushion. The features of the face have been somewhat damaged in the course of time.

The Piper Choir

The North Choir Aisle or Piper Choir and the Vestry

THE NORTH CHOIR aisle has for some time been known as the Piper choir, though the invaluable Church Book shows that it was also, perhaps earlier, termed "the Organ Quire". There seems little doubt that the "paire of organs of great valewe"[165] which Mr George Preston presented to the church in the early seventeenth century stood at the west end of this chapel against the screen, part of which is left uncarved, in contrast to the rest. Whether the name of the choir derives from the organ pipes or from the fact that members of the Pepper family were buried here, or for some other reason, it is impossible to tell.

Almost all the present chapel belongs to the original structure and must be dated somewhere in or near the first decade of the thirteenth century, apart from the two windows in its north wall which were inserted in the mid-fifteenth century. These are made of red sandstone and were probably imported from Furness; they have what are the only known mason's marks in the church. The choir has a quadripartite vault with simple chamfered ribs, which can safely claim to be the oldest roofing extant in Southern Lakeland. As we have seen, the outer orders of the adjoining two great semi-circular arches on its south side and those of the narrow pointed arch at its western end are decorated only with simple chamfers, in sharp contrast to the richly decorated faces on the inner sides of the church. Originally the chapel had a lancet window of the stock type in its eastern wall but this no longer exists.

Although the Piper Choir, like the Town Choir, has lost every trace of its medieval altar, in its easternmost pier may be seen a shallow niche for a statue and close to it remains of a small piscina. Nearby, set in the floor adjoining the north wall, is a large and handsome tombstone with a neatly carved cross, in the head of which is shown a chalice. In the corner near it stand two very crudely carved loose tombstones, one of which was shortened to serve as a doorstep in the village in post-medieval times. Close by, on the south side of the floor of the chapel, is another tombstone of grey limestone of more conventional design, also having a chalice carved on it. In the westernmost of the two windows in the north wall are two small panels of 15th century glass in poor condition, depicting St. Gregory and St. Jerome, two of the Doctors of the Church.

In the fifteenth century a small sacristy was added to the east end of the Piper Choir. This adjoined the sanctuary to which it had direct access by a small door in its south wall, which is now blocked up and which lost some of its original height when, for no very good reason, the Victorians raised the level of the sanctuary floor here. After the suppression of the priory much of the local responsibilities of the government of the vast parish so far as social and administrative affairs were concerned, passed into the hands of a body of local men known as "the Twenty Four". For their meetings the old sacristy was much too small, but this problem of space was solved by the piety and wealth of Mr William Robinson of Newby Bridge who, as his massive memorial by the vestry door records, "eternised his name by building the vestry at Cartmel". His will of 1677 bequeathed the then considerable sum of £40 for building "a new vestry and questhouse over the same...the present vestry being a small and low building and unproportionable to the rest of the said church".[166] As a result a most admirable transformation was effected. A larger building was erected on the site with two storeys with a roof, which to some degree matched that of the Town Choir, and had an east wall in line with those of chancel and Town Choir, thus producing a most satisfying unity of design which has delighted innumerable artists down the years. This unity is increased by the fact that much old stone was re-used. A fifteenth century window which was perhaps in the original sacristy, was inserted in the new east wall; it retains a small panel of contemporary glass depicting St. John the Evangelist. (It is a very curious fact that the east front of the prior church which, if viewed superficially, appears to be largely of one date, consists of work of four different periods – the thirteenth, fourteenth, fifteenth and seventeenth centuries). The new vestry was a capacious room on the first floor of the new edifice. It was entered by a small door in its western wall reached by a short staircase, and lit by the attractive fifteenth century window, whose original location is uncertain. The unlovely chamber beneath the vestry is now a stoke-hole. The minute books of the meetings of the Twenty Four which were held here date from 1597, and as Stockdale showed, are of immense value for the local historian. They are now in the County Record Office at Kendal.

The Transepts, Crossing and Belfry

The Northern Transept

AS HAS BEEN SEEN, the walls of the north transept are part of the first building scheme. They were probably built towards the end of this, i.e. in the earliest decades of the thirteenth century. The north wall originally had four lancet windows arranged in pairs. When the cloisters were moved to the north side of the church in the fifteenth century, the top pair of lancets were replaced by a single window of five lights and the lower two blocked up, the western one of these two having now inserted in it the old dormitory door which had originally been in the corresponding position in the south transept. This re-utilisation of an old piece of work instead of creating a modern one in the latest architectural style is an unusual medieval development – was it due to asceticism or financial stringency or both?

In the east wall of the north transept is a similar curiosity – a largish window whose head is a four-pointed arch of a type not to be found before the fifteenth century, but which was here entirely constructed with early thirteenth century stonework, probably from the materials of the twin lancets which it replaced, the outer jambs of these with their elegant shafts remaining *in situ*. In the north west corner of the transept a small door affords entrance to the vice which leads up to a wall passage which goes round the transept, and gives access to the area over the vault of the Piper Choir. The floor of the transept is now largely covered by Victorian pews, below one of which almost certainly remains a slab inscribed HIS DEUM ADORA ("Here adore God"), mentioned in an old guide book – (perhaps the Blessed Sacrament was reserved at the altar here). It is unlikely that this area was greatly used by the local congregations, the south transept, Town Choir, crossing and nave more than sufficing for the usual attendance. The small doorway over the western arch of the transept, was probably built in preparation for an early aisled nave which was never completed in full. The removal of the cloisters to the north side of the nave entailed the blocking of the lower part of the lancet window in the west wall of this transept, by the lean-to cloister roof outside, but the demolition of the cloister at the Reformation meant that the window once again gave complete light – it is now the only one of the original windows of the priory still fulfilling its pristine function. In the eastern and western walls of both transepts just above the arches leading into the aisles are small doorways with early filling.

The Crossing and Belfry

THE FOUR MASSIVE piers of the crossing with their clustered columns are all part of the original building programme of the monastery but were repaired in or about the early fifteenth century. The capitals of their arches are simple ones with no elaborate decoration. The wood ceiling is a Victorian one (1850) and bears the arms of the arch-diocese of York, the diocese of Chester (to which the priory pertained from 1541 to 1836), the arms of the priory itself and those of its great benefactor, George Preston of Holker. The circular cavity in the centre exists, of course, to facilitate the transport of bells. The very fine brass candelabra was presented by Mrs Margaret Marshall of Aynsome in 1734.

We have no evidence of any kind to show us the appearance of the original belfry of the priory. It presumably stood on the site of the present lantern, which has now some original work but was extensively

The Crossing

reconstructed in the fifteenth century. Wooden belfries were not unknown in medieval England, and it is possible that a poorish priory like Cartmel originally had one of these at first. It is certainly remarkable that the present one is built diagonally across the lantern tower, with very massive retaining arches beneath to support it. Why was this?

I am most indebted to Mr T. J. Green, British Railways Civil Engineer, for the invaluable following comments on this special configuration of the present belfry of Cartmel priory which gives it such an unusual external appearance:

"The upper section of the Bell Tower is a square, the sides of which lie in the north-west, south-east, the north-east and south-west directions. The lower section is a larger square with sides lying north, south, west and east. The lower section is conventional, inasmuch as its geometry is consistant with north, south and east, west configuration of the main priory building which supports it. The upper section is not conventional, lying as it does at 45 degrees to the lower section. The upper section is founded on the mid-points of the sides of the lower square section. The suggestion that the smaller upper section was built this way on economic grounds has to be challenged. Less materials were necessary to build the upper smaller square section than would have been used if the lower larger section had been built to the full height required. However, the additional labour costs and the extra cost of temporary supports to build the peculiar upper section would have outweighed the costs of materials saved. It is a moot point anyway as to whether economic considerations would have prevailed at the time the tower was built. It is necessary to seek a more cogent explanation. I do so as an engineer rather than as an expert in ecclesiastical architecture. One factor which could provide an explanation is that the upper section of the tower is lighter than it would have been if the lower section had been continued to full height. The ground upon which the Priory is founded is not good and indeed it is suggested that there was a history of foundation problems towards the south side of the site. Whilst the upper tower section is lighter, the reduction in weight is unlikely to have made a significant contribution to any foundation problems: the weight-saving motive is rejected therefore.

Other evidence has to be sought. There is evidence, still to be seen, upon which a plausible explanation can be based. The lower tower is supported on each of its four sides on walls which are spandrels to major arches. These spandrel walls are cracked and appear to have been cracked for many years. The crack pattern is such that it appears that the arches were bursting upwards. This phenomenon is not uncommon. The design of arches and the spandrel walls they support was and remains an inexact science. Even in Roman times the arch builders had bursting failures which can be caused by failing to achieve the proper size of spandrel wall to suit the shape of arch chosen. This may have been the case at Cartmel. The spandrel walls may have started to crack and the arch may have started to burst upwards during the construction period. The mason would have been aware of this failure mode and he would have had to seek a remedial solution. The remedy for an arch which is bursting upwards is to load the crown of the arch. By rotating the upper tower through forty-five degrees and making the upper section with arches enabled him to point load the major arches below with all the weight of the upper section of the tower. By doing this he successfully arrested the cracking of the spandrels and the tendency for the major arches below to burst upwards. The peculiar bell tower at Cartmel may therefore be a splendid example of the engineering excellence of the mason who built it."

Petit, from his wide experience, knew of no other diagonal central belfry of this type in England and only one in France – at Rheims.

The Bells

UNLIKE THE LATER history of Cartmel's bells, that of their medieval times is undocumented. In 1536 there was stated to be three large bells and four small ones belonging to the monastery and three others claimed by the parishioners.[167] None of the existing bells are very old, considerable re-casting having gone on down the centuries as the Church Book shows us. For long the church relied on four bells, two of 1661, one of 1726, one of 1729. These having become sub-standard were joined by four new ones in 1987.[167]

The South Transept

THE SOUTH TRANSEPT, like its northern neighbour, is part of the original building programme of the priory church, and probably dates from the years just after 1200. It is an excellent example of the so-called Transitional style, built with the attractive stone from Quarry Flat. It has been very little altered apart from its fenestration and roof timbers. At the north end of its east wall is the entrance to the Town Choir, with its pointed head of three orders vigorously if rather roughly carved. Above is a small round-headed door which gave access both to the wall passage which runs round the transept at this level, and to the roof of the Town Choir. The widening of the latter meant that the original window in the east wall of the transept had to be destroyed. It was replaced by an unlovely, smaller one with the curious splayed sides demanded by the cramped space available, its northern jamb being cut across the thickness of the new south wall of the Town Choir. In the south wall of the transept is a short flight of steps which leads to the circular stair in its south east corner; by which there is access both to the wall passages and to the roof, whence a small door leads to the path to the bell-ringing chamber. Also in the south wall are two mid-fifteenth century windows of medium size, one of five lights the other of six, which were inserted here after the cloister buildings of the priory had been moved from the south to the north side of the church. Originally, at the western end of the south wall at first floor level, as was usual, was the doorway which connected the dormitory with the church by a stair, but in order to give access to the new dormitory this doorway was moved to the corresponding position in the north transept, where it still remains; it has typical Transitional traits, its semi-circular head being combined with early Gothic mouldings. The glass of the windows here is Victorian and like the rest of the glass of this period in the church is the work of Shrigley and Hunt of Lancaster. In a corner of the transept here there has recently been placed an exhibition case which contains, amongst other things, a very old and cumbersome umbrella with wooden ribs and a painted canvas cover, thought to have been given for use by the incumbent when conducting burials in the rain. Here also are a few of the small objects found in the Harrington tomb when it was opened over a century ago.

In the west wall there was originally a small semi-circular headed window placed just above the line of the old cloister roof, to give badly

The South Transept

needed light here, since the south wall of the transept was originally largely blocked by adjacent buildings. In 1624 this small window was blocked by the insertion of a new clock with dials showing the time both within and without the church.[168] The west wall of the transept divided the church from the northern end of the eastern alley to the cloister. The ruthless establishment of Victorian pews all over the south transept prevents us from knowing whether its floor contains any interesting ancient tombstones. In the west wall of the transept, over the Transitional archway which links it with the nave, is another small doorway. It has a pointed head, not a semi-circular one like the one facing it in the opposite wall; on the other side of it are set two curious stone knobs perhaps intended to hold a beam to be used in hauling up building material. The nature and size of the early nave of the priory is totally unknown, but it is quite likely that aisles which were planned for it were not completed for a very long time. The clerestory of both transepts consisted only of a pair of small rectangular windows in each of its eastern and western walls.

The only memorial of special interest now visible here is a late Elizabethan one in memory of one of the Thornburgh family of Hampsfield Hall and his wife, both of whom were almost certainly "Church-papist" (i.e. nominally Anglican but attending Roman Catholic worship). This reads:–

> Here before lyeth interred
> Etheldred Thornburgh corps in dust
> In lyfe at death styll fyrmely fixed
> On God to rest hir stedfast trust
> Hir father Justice Carus was
> Hir mother Katharine his wiffe
> Hir husband William Thornburgh was
> Whylst here she ledd this mortall lyfe
> The third of Martche and year of grace
> One thousand fyve hundred nyntie six
> Hir sowle departed this earthly plase
> Of aage nighe fortie years and six
> To whose sweet sowle heavenlye dwellinge
> Our Saviour grant everlastinge

(The coat of arms originally at the top of this monument has unhappily been erased). It is interesting to note that the inscription ends with a prayer for the soul of the deceased person, (a thing not approved in Anglican public worship at the time) and that the original Etheldreda was an Anglo-Saxon abbess.

The North Side of the Nave

The Nave

THERE IS NEXT to no evidence to show us the dimensions of the first nave of the church which, as we have seen, was probably built in the early half of the thirteenth century, but was almost totally destroyed when the present structure was constructed in the first half of the fifteenth century. It was certainly short, and may have lacked one or both aisles, or had only very short ones. The main clearly recognisable relic of the early building here is the very fine Transitional door in the east end of the south wall. This was originally either intended to connect the church with the cloister or (less likely) to serve as the west door of the first nave. It is round-headed and of three orders, with some mouldings of Romanesque type, though its detached shafts with their rather crudely carved stiff-leaf foliage have an early Gothic look. This door was probably one of the first adjuncts of the new priory church to be constructed. Although the small arches over the two eastern entrances to the aisles of the present nave show that it was from the first intended to have twin aisles there, it is worthy of note that these small arches are blocked with what seems to be contemporary ashlar. This suggests that, because of lack of money (possibly due to the death of the founder of the priory in 1219) it was decided not to give the nave any aisles, but make do, at least temporarily, with an aisleless one which was probably quite short. The line of the original west wall of this nave is totally unknown, and remains of it may well have been largely destroyed by the extensive burials in the nave after the dissolution of the priory.

The present outer walls of the nave are very largely of early fifteenth century date though the portion immediately west of the cloister door was evidently reconstructed in the seventeenth century. At the western end of the north wall of the nave is a substantial piece of walling some fifty feet long and five feet high which, rather oddly, projects a little from the rest of the wall, which it clearly pre-dates. Perhaps the most likely explanation of this is that it was originally part of a separate building which stood to the north-west of an original small aisleless nave, and was incorporated in the later (present) one without total accuracy.

The nave is unusual in having no less than four doorways:–

1. The great doorway at the east end of the south wall which, as we have noted, perhaps originally communicated with the monastic cloister, and which, when the latter was moved to the north side of the church, was probably retained as the main entrance for the parishioners and almost certainly had a porch put round it, (which was necessary for use in medieval marriage ceremonies). But, as the *Old Church Book* shows us, the porch was ordered to be rebuilt in 1626 "in the same place where formerlye it was...the wall to be

**The
South Door**

rayses upp, as the west syde and a new roufe to be made over it and a
frees-stone doore with an arche."[169]

2. At the west end of the south wall of the nave is a modest doorway of
mid-fifteenth century date. This would provide a subsidiary entrance, principally for those worshipping in the nave, the south
transept and south choir aisle, all of which, as we have seen, by a
very unusual arrangement, were used by the parishioners. This
entrance retains its original traceried wooden door, very little
damaged. It is known as "the Cromwell door'. (If tradition is
correct, this is because, when the Cromwellian soldiers visited the
church in 1643, they stabled their horses in its nave, leading
indignant locals to fire at the then closed door hereby causing what
are said to be bullet holes (which are still very visible).

97

3. In the west wall of the nave, unsymmetrically placed beneath the great west window, is a very minor doorway barely five feet high with a simple lintel as its head. This was for the private use of the prior, his household and guests and gave access to the church across a small enclosed courtyard from the prior's house. The latter still stands, albeit no little altered, on the west side of the yard that adjoins the west end of the church. The west end of the church was increased in size by the construction of a small post-Reformation annex which is said to have served as a bone-hole, which is likely enough, given the popularity of burial here.

4. At the east end of the north wall of the nave is a large and very elegant doorway which must be dated to the second quarter of the 13th century or thereabouts. Externally it is of three orders, each having detached shafts and some dog-tooth ornament. It is very likely indeed, though it cannot be proved, that this was originally the west door of the midget-sized nave first constructed for the priory. It was almost certainly moved to its present position when the cloister buildings of the house were moved from the south to the north side of the church to give easy access between the cloister and the church. It is still in excellent condition.

The windows of the present nave are mostly not impressive. In the south wall towards its western end are two with four-pointed heads probably made fairly late in the 15th century. The west wall has a fairly large window as its centre piece, also in conventional latish 15th century style and flanked by adjoining minor windows. The north aisle wall has no windows because the southern alley of the later cloister adjoined it. The new nave was not provided with a triforium, almost certainly for financial reasons, and its clerestory windows are small and humble – only two on either side, of simple rectangular design with only two lights.

Inside, on the north wall of the nave, at its western end, are hatchments of the Lowther and Cavendish families of the 18th and 19th centuries, and an earlier painted memorial panel to the Preston family which gives some interesting details of its benefactions. Further west is a monument to Lord Frederick Cavendish, with its noble effigy of white marble carved by Thomas Woolner and exhibited at the Royal Academy in 1885 before being installed here. Near the Cromwell door is an attractive, modern sculpture in bronze of "The Flight into Egypt", by Mrs Josephine Vasconcellas. Like most of the rest of the church the nave acquired from George Preston, a most attractive plaster ceiling, which for good reasons or bad, was removed by the Victorians; ancient prints show us its resemblance to similar work in the main rooms at Levens Hall and Sizergh Castle. In the floor of the nave are a number of post-Reformation tombstones. The quaint memorial to Mr Rowland Briggs of Swallowmire

The South Wall of the Nave

now against the north west pier of the crossing not only records his bequest of £20 "to be laid out in bread and distributed to the most indigent house-keepers of this parish every Sunday for ever" (a charity still maintained) but also a payment of 5s to be paid every Christmas Day to the Sexton, provided his grave remained "unbroken up".

The Building Stone of the Church

THE BUILDING STONE of the present priory church of Cartmel has recently been fully investigated by Mr Murray Mitchell, late of the Geological Survey, on whose work the following notes are based. His investigation confirmed that the old local tradition, handed down to the present writer by his grandmother, is perfectly correct in claiming that the original priory church here was constructed with stone from the quarry at Quarry Flat. This has long been dis-used and the construction of the nearby railway led to reclamation of land which deprived the quarry of the access to the waters of the estuary which it had hitherto enjoyed. Almost certainly the building stone for the priory was transported by water up Cark Beck (which was then a great deal wider and deeper than it is now) probably as far as the Inn there, and then taken by land to Cartmel, probably along the Birkby road.

Mr Mitchell's analysis of the stone has shown that the stone used in the parts of the church built before the fifteenth century is of three kinds:–

(i)   Sandstone B –   pale grey or almost white; extensively used for interior decorative work.
(ii) Sandstone C –   hardwearing, so successfully used for windows, sills mullions and drip courses.
(iii) Sandstone D –   used extensively for the general exterior work.

It is most interesting and unexpected to find that in this isolated area at so early a date the builders of Cartmel priory were fully aware of the distinctive characteristics of the three types of sandstone which they employed with conspicuous success. As to the present nave, which as we have seen, was built in the fifteenth century, much later than the rest of the church, Mitchell points out that "it shows a totally different style of construction from the use of well-masoned blocks from Quarry Flat... Random use is made of undressed blocks of limestone, mainly from the Red Hill Oolite and Dalton beds, with blocks of Bannisdale Slate and cobbles of Lower Palaeozoic, volcanic and sedimentary rocks from the drift. Much of this material must have been derived from small quarries and diggings in the immediate vicinity of Cartmel".

THE DOMESTIC BUILDINGS OF THE PRIORY

IN PRE-REFORMATION days the conventual church of Cartmel was accompanied by the usual considerable variety of buildings great and small, scattered inside a large monastic precinct that was bounded by a very substantial wall, of which very little is now visible, though portions of it are incorporated in various houses in the present village. The fate of these domestic buildings of the priory after the Dissolution varied very considerably. Some have disappeared completely, but the walls of a few others have been extensively incorporated in later buildings, though the original doors and windows, with one minor exception, have disappeared. Alone of the major domestic buildings of the priory, the gatehouse still retains much of its original appearance. Very early in the priory's history, these buildings were laid out according to a very careful and intelligent plan, in three clear-cut areas, separated from each other on the west by the river Ay (the only substantial water supply in the area) which ran southward, and on the east by an anonymous little beck which, rather curiously, runs in the opposite direction.

(i) The western of these divisions was largely devoted to the maintenance of various social responsibilities of the monastery, and was dominated by the great gatehouse, where local justice was dispensed, and which guarded the main public entrance to the monastic precinct. Through its massive entrance arch a little street ran north, having along its sides brewery, bakery, and very extensive accommodation of the simple kind to which medieval folk were accustomed, much of which has now disappeared through having become superfluous once the priory had gone. Underlying this area lay Bannisdale slate which gave the surest of foundations, but allowed no cellarage to the buildings above.

(ii) The central area of the monastic precinct was dominated by the monastic church, on one side of which nestled the cloister, hedged around by the usual major buildings, which like the cloister itself, have disappeared completely, probably through being sold off for building material at the Dissolution by the new owner Thomas Holcroft, to whom money mattered very greatly. Here also, adjoining the north and south sides of the church, were twin cemeteries, one for the parishioners, the other for the monastic community.

(iii) The eastern sector mostly served agricultural purposes, though here also, easily accessible without disturbing monastic peace, were the dwellings allotted to the parish clergy. This area lay outside the main monastic precinct with its great wall. At its northern end was the

101

mighty "great barn" with a smaller barn and a variety of allied structures nearby. Further south, in the angle where the old road north to Newton met the little causeway made by the priory was the home farm. Here was a small farmhouse with a small barn attached, behind which was a farm yard probably lined with now vanished shippons and the like, whilst in the adjoining field on the west was evidently a largish dairy. If at the Dissolution a well-to-do squire had bought the priory site and resided therein, much of this complex might have remained, but as this was not so the reverse was the case.

The Cloister

A MEDIEVAL MONASTIC cloister was almost always square in plan and consisted of four broad corridors with lean-to-roofs abutting on the various buildings which surrounded its outer sides and having an open garth in the middle thereof. At Cartmel, as we have seen, by an action which may well have been unique in medieval England, round about the end of the fourteenth century the expensive and elaborate decision was taken to transfer the cloister with its attendant buildings from the south side of the church to a corresponding position on the north side, with the curious result that the north wall of the north transept and the south wall of the south transept now both contain a blocked recess for a dormitory door and their west walls both retain a few of the corbels which supported the roof of former eastern alleys of cloister. Apart from this we have no visible signs at all of the cloisters and the complex of domestic buildings connected with them. The first (southern) cloister was destroyed long before the Dissolution and the second one almost immediately after it. The fact that the area covered by the second cloister was later much used for interments in post-Reformation days almost certainly means that informative old foundations there no longer exist.

On the eastern side of the later cloister, aligned with the north transept, there would have been a two-storey building, its lower floor separated from the transept by a narrow passage which had over it a small bridge that gave access to a door (still visible, albeit blocked up) from which steps led down into the church. Most of the upper floor of the block was taken up by the monastic dormitory. From the ground floor beneath, adjoining a passage, a largish room projected eastwards. This was the chapter house, which had a longish chamber running at right angles to it, in line with the nearby transept. The northern side of the cloister here would have been largely taken up by a spacious refectory, which had the high table at its eastern end and hatches in the wall at its western one, through which food and dishes were passed from the adjacent kitchen. It is possible but not certain that, like the refectory still intact at Carlisle cathedral, that at Cartmel had a vaulted undercroft beneath it.

The western side of the cloister would have been enclosed by a two storey building which, amongst other things, probably contained a small set of rooms for the prior at its northern or southern end and accommodation for ecclesiastical guests nearby. The south side of the later cloister, of course, adjoined the north wall of the nave of the church, in the outer face of which may still be seen some very scanty and crude relics of the cloister roof – a dripstone and corbels which are nothing more than unworked chunks of slate, most inferior in appearance to the carefully carved ones which are usually found in this position.

The Priory Close

NEARBY, OUTSIDE THE western side of the churchyard, is now a smallish two-storey building which is almost certainly all of post-Reformation date and has very recently been refurbished. West of it is a longish narrow yard, till recently all cobbled, which has towards its southern end a gateway marked Priory Close. This is almost certainly in a very ancient position, and marks the original boundary between the private grounds of the priory and the outside world. Along the western side of this yard runs a long building which, together with the adjoining wing at its southern end, forms a large and important unit. Its walls have been given very post-medieval doors and windows. There is no doubt that this L-shaped building was originally built as a single unit in medieval times – probably in the first half of the fifteenth century, as part of the very extensive architectural reorganisation which followed the re-building of the cloister on a new site. Although the medieval windows are no longer visible, traces of them may yet exist beneath the roughcast. Most of the medieval walling and parts of the old roof timbers and floor yet remain; in post-Reformation times the interior here was extensively modernised.

The eastern wing is now dominated by a central section having a lofty front which was probably extended to its present height in Georgian times. Its central passage has a very spacious room on either side and is doubtless of medieval origin, as are the stairs to the upper floor behind it, but it is quite impossible to decide the extent of medieval work yet remaining. This area probably provided the accommodation for high ranking guests such as bishops, archdeacons and nobility such as the Harringtons. It is adjoined on the north side by a small modest set of rooms which may be the much altered prior's apartments and are notable for having retained on the first floor a small stone doorway with pointed head, certainly of late medieval date, which is the only one known of this antiquity in Cartmel; the door is still in use, but what was probably the circular stair which led up to it has gone. The northern end of the range has been very extensively altered at various times and presents an archaeological puzzle. Further south, the corner area at the junction of the two wings of this block is now a shop and has been very extensively altered in modern times. The present entrance here, which faces south, until comparatively recently led to a narrow passage, in both of whose side walls were not very large doors. That on the east side led to what was probably a sizeable living room, remains of whose substantial fireplace and chimney are visable from outside.

The range extends westward by what was probably a separable element. It has its own door, and is of three storeys. Inside there happily yet remain *in situ* two pairs of the tall crutches used in a few other medieval dwellings elsewhere in the village. Parts of the floors here consist of 3ins thick boards almost certainly of medieval date. In the north wall of this block are four small oblong windows set at ascending heights and now blocked up, which probably provided light for a small but now vanished stair. We can only guess who used this living space, but some of the numerous servants of the priory and attendants of major guests may well have done so. The land adjoining this wing on the north may have been used for stabling, stores and a yard. Across the beck, westward from this block, lies the very minor village square, which is dominated by the gatehouse which was originally linked on either side to a substantial precinct wall, now mostly gone or lost in later housing. Like the buildings which line the street north of the gatehouse and like the western side of the precinct wall (of which little is here visible though substantial portions exist in some of the later houses) this area stands on a great outcrop of Bannisdale slate, which provided very stable foundations. The market place here has never been significant. Cartmel village down the ages has been too isolated and the local population much too small to support any significant trade, though for long fish-stones near the cross stump must have served to display much valued fish from the nearby bay. One or two of the houses here are ancient but have been much modernised.

The Gatehouse

IT IS UNFORTUNATELY quite impossible to identify the site of the original gatehouse or priory and the subsidiary buildings which adjoined it. Quite probably it was nowhere near the existing building, which may well be an afterthought of the 14th century. For obvious reasons of convenience the normal position of a medieval monastic gatehouse was close to its conventual church and facing its western front, where the main public entrance of the latter was normally to be found. As we have seen, geological reasons made monastery building at Cartmel much more difficult than usual, but the original gatehouse may have been somewhere quite close to the west end of the church with its original, very undersized

The Gatehouse of Cartmel Priory

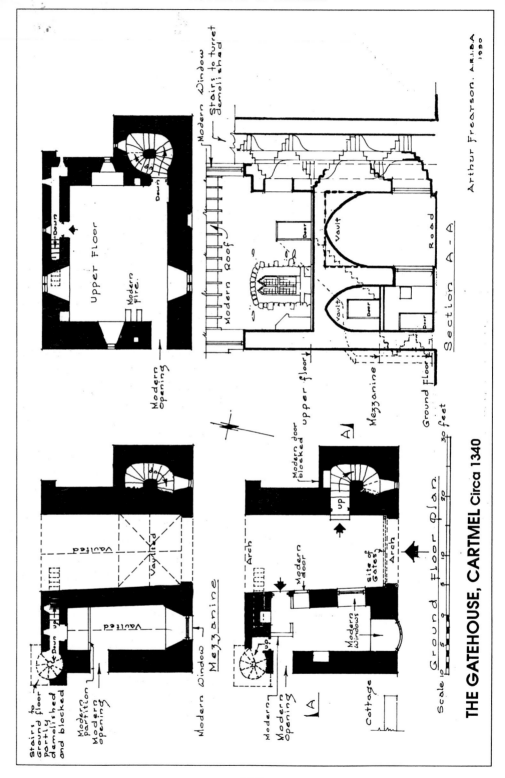

THE GATEHOUSE, CARTMEL Circa 1340

nave, but of it no trace remains.

The present gatehouse faces south and is entered through a large arched passage 12ft wide and 24ft long. The great outer arch is of simple construction and has over it a moulded rectangular recess presumably for a statue. The entrance passage is jointly roofed by a crude pointed barrel vault and a groined quadripartite one. In its east wall is a small door, somewhat altered, from which a series of roughly made and very uneven steps lead to the courtroom above, which engrosses the whole of the first floor. Originally the most important use of this was as the manorial court-room, a function which it continued to perform after the Dissolution. Two of the post-Reformation court books of Cartmel have survived in the Bodleian Library, Oxford and three others in the Public Record Office in London.[170] In 1624 the place was bought to become the school[171] of the area, a purpose for which it was far from ideal. Changes then made included the insertion of a largish window in each of the two gables and the addition of a small loft in its eastern end. The virtual demolition of the turret at its south east corner and the replacement of the old battlements along with the rebuilding of the roof evidently also belong to this period. In 1791 the trustees having found the building place "awkward and difficult", sold it to James Stockdale, the purchase money being assigned towards the purchase of a new school.[172] In 1807 Mr Stockdale junior and his wife sold the place to Robert Galloway of Cartmel, saddler, whose children sold it to James Field of Cartmel[173] who may have been responsible for the insertion of a door and window in the southwest corner of the tower and a door in the adjoining east wall in order to make this area into a shop, a function which it filled until comparatively recently. It is said that in Victorian days the great courtroom was used as a Methodist chapel and later as a billiard room, for neither of which purposes can it have been ideal.

In course of time the place fell into serious decay. From this state it was rescued by the late Mr R. O'Neill Person who, having restored it magnificently, at no little expense, presented it to the National Trust in 1922. In modern times no permanent purpose has been found for the court-room, but it occasionally houses exhibitions of various kinds.

The court-room measures 17ft by 17ft 5ins internally. In its western wall is a little damaged medieval fireplace with a small window nearby, and a niche. At the western ends of the north and south walls are a pair of fourteenth century windows. These are of two lights with transoms and trefoiled heads, and have stone benches at either side. The rest of the south wall is blank but the northern one has at its west end a largish wall cupboard. Further east of it is a small square-headed door that leads to a wall stair which would provide access to the court-room from the monastic precincts; and which has lost its steps. Adjoining the head of the stair is a very small chamber which was probably a very elementary *châlet de necessité.* The main entrance to the court-room from the external stair is at the southern end of the eastern wall; close to it is a niche which may have held a crucifix. (Plan p.106).

The street which ran northward from the gatehouse is now known as Cavendish Street, a title probably only acquired some two centuries ago when the family of that name inherited the extensive estates centred on Holker Hall, most of which had originally belonged to the priory. Originally the street was principally bordered by buildings used in the very extensive hospitality offered by the priory to the travelling public. Here was the main guest-house later converted into a large inn and known in latish times as the Cavendish Arms. Adjoining its south side is a large building originally made to contain the beers since cellarage was not possible here because of the Bannisdale slate beneath – (Bread and beer constituted the staple medieval diet). The bread for the guests was quite certainly made in the corner house just across the road from the inn; in it an immensely antique brick bee-hive shaped oven, which may well have been of medieval date, remained until about half a century ago. After the Dissolution this place continued to provide food, being known as "Ye Old Eating House" in the present writer's childhood. Much of the land between it and the gatehouse was for long largely taken up by an orchard. The small path that adjoins the eating house, probably led originally to a few small houses just inside the boundary wall – the age of those now in this area is very uncertain. It is possible, but not proven, that when the first nàve was built, a rough paved road led from its main door down to the river and crossed it by a bridge, to terminate in or near Cavendish Street.

Of the houses bordering the north western end of Cavendish Street little is known though some of these are probably mentioned, without being identifiable in the Holker Hall deeds, of which an invaluable calendar has been published. Here reference is made to "the Great House or Guest Stable"[174] which may well have adjoined the north side of the Cavendish Arms and which at times probably provided nourishment below with sleeping accommodation above for a largish number of people. Adjoining it, and in the large yard behind the Cavendish Arms, was probably additional accommodation of an elementary type for man and beast – (it is to be noted that at the Dissolution the great value of the hospitality dispensed by the monasteries in our area was stressed and that in times of crisis Cartmel priory was bound to produce a largish contingent of men to fight the intolerable Scots, which might have to be temporarily accommodated). In the attic of the Cavendish Arms are still to be seen some remains of a cockpit. Cockfighting was, of course, for long a favourite English pastime and lingered on in South Cumbria much later than in most other parts of England. Cocks were still being bred in the Cartmel area in the present writer's boyhood, and surreptitious cockfighting was not extinct in South Cumbria.

At the north east corner of Cavendish Street is a cramped building which for many years was a smithy used both for shoeing horses and for making and fitting the iron rims for cartwheels so very valuable in this rough countryside. The process of manufacture was concluded by the new wheel being pushed down the adjacent little slope into the beck to cool and contract. At this point the public road turns eastward over a large, fairly new bridge which replaced what was originally a small one, which gave access to the private grounds of the monastery.

The Infirmary

THIS ROAD HAS on its northern side, opposite the church, a small field which is of substantial archaeological interest. It is called "farmery" field, this being the old word for what we call today the infirmary. This edifice was an essential element in a medieval monastery, providing the necessarily private treatment for sick and infirm brethren. Air photos show that it followed the stock plan of such things, the main element being a large hall with twin aisles and an open area at one end. In Cartmel this structure ran north and south, and had running out from its eastern side a subsidiary block which probably accommodated necessary stores and quarters for the infirmarer who was in charge of the place. To the north, some fifty yards from the road, as air photos show clearly, was a broad ditch which, with a fence, helped to guard the privacy of the place. As 17th century documents show us, all or part of the auxiliary wing was retained at the Dissolution, but later fell into decay for unknown reasons. It is very much to be hoped that before too long this interesting area will receive that full scientific excavation that modern learning provides.

On the east side of farmery field ran part of the boundary of the monastic precinct, probably made of walling, though a hedge adjoining a now vanished pond may have served here originally. At the point where its southern end met the road that runs eastward there was almost certainly a small side-gatehouse which was largely for the private use of the brethren once their cloisters had been moved to this side of the church; it also gave easy access to the part of the cemetery which adjoined the eastern side of the church which was probably used for the burial of inmates of the priory. It is an interesting illustration of local conservatism that for long after the Dissolution this former monastic entrance to the churchyard was not used for public funerals. On the north side of this entrance, on what is now a public road, there is now a group of three cottages, the western two, which were evidently made out of an already existing building of very uncertain age and purpose; behind them is a field which slopes down to a beck. The area to the north is very low-lying and liable to flooding; originally it was part of the thin lake that ran from Newton to Headless Cross. Opposite, adjoining the south side of the road is a small, very low-lying field, very given to flooding, which may have had the monastic fishponds, though Dr Mitchell finds an area some hundred yards higher up the beck more likely for these.

As we have noted, in this area, along the eastern side of the field which adjoins the east side of the church and the main cemetery runs a small stream which, unlike the beck on the west side of the church, runs northward not southward. Just below the point where it crosses the road from the infirmary, it provides a small but most noble spring which never runs dry and provides the purest water. The small path which leads to it almost certainly goes back to monastic days and has a public right of way; till recent times the well was much used by nearby residents. The road adjoining it on the north is Priests' Lane and proceeds eastward to join the very ancient road that goes northward to Newton and southward to Headless Cross whence it divides to reach the villages in the south of the valley. The road's title derives from the fact that the two semi-detached houses which adjoin it some fifty yards from the well were the very conveniently placed dwellings allotted to the secular clergy on whom the main charge of the parishioners of the area devolved. As these were the main users of the wells in medieval days it came to acquire its present title of Priests' Well.

The semi-detached houses at the north east corner of Barngarth, like several of the houses in the village, are a great deal older than they look, though as their original doors and windows have been mostly completely modernised and their walls covered with roughcast without and plaster within; it is mostly not feasible to date them. The southernmost of these two is much less altered than its outward appearance suggests. Its windows are not ancient (there is no medieval window still intact in the village) but most of the structure has not been significantly altered and it has the stock plan of several medieval priests' houses in England. A very medieval characteristic is the passage going from the front entrance across the middle of the house breadth-ways — the so-called "screens passage". The north side of this has a stout wall probably of mediaval date; on its south side is a wooden screen, to which a 16th century date is given. At the end of the passage a projecting circular stair leads to the upper floor, though this has been extensively re-modelled in post-medieval times. On either side of this passage is a living room. There are slight signs that these two rooms and the corresponding ones next door were united by a broadish passage along their eastern sides bounded by a thin wooden partition of which a little remains. Both the houses have useful sized gardens which, in medieval times especially, had much privacy through being in the monastic precinct. The entrance door of the northern house, like its interior, was extensively modernised in fairly

110

recent times. That of its southern partner has jambs much of which may be medieval, include a piece of battered dog-tooth ornament. Inside it are two enormous iron hinges *in situ* which probably supported the medieval door. It is very likely, though unprovable, that these are the buildings which a deed of 1576 calls "Sir Oliver's houses",[176] since from 1506 onward until at least 1536 Oliver Levyns was the parish priest of Cartmel and holders of this office were long known by this title. The fact that the two yew trees which flank the entrance of the northern house were, until recently, known as "Peter" and "Emma", after an 18th century incumbent called Peter Richardson and his wife, suggests that this place was the usual residence for clergy for a very long while.

There is little evidence of any kind to show what buildings stood in the medieval Priests' Lane. A document of 1509 mentions shops there,[177] which must have been few and small and were probably on its south side. It is possible that on the other side of Priests' Lane in medieval times was a small local prison, which much more recently was temporarily refurbished as a Police Station. The small yard in this area contains some good thirteenth century carved stones whose original home is uncertain; they may have originally belonged to a small gatehouse which must have existed adjacent to the southernmost priest's house to guard access to barns and other attendant structures in this area. The present road which runs the length of Barngarth is very unlikely to have existed as more than a very minor track in monastic days, and even this is uncertain.

Barngarth

IN PRE-REFORMATION DAYS almost certainly these two houses and the road on the north formed two sides of a small open yard, which had on its south side a strong gateway and on the west the northern end of the huge structure which deeds call "the Great Barne",[178] the last remains of which totally disappeared some considerable time ago. Unhappily we know little precise about its dimensions; it was certainly an imposing and complex structure whose north end probably formed part of the south wall of the small passage which led to Priest's Well. Almost certainly it was very long and very wide (having twin aisles) and had apparently some shippons beneath the main floor, probably where the ground on the west side slopes down to the beck. It is likely but unprovable that the straight line of the beck here was artificially created by the brethren principally to provide a source of water to use in case of fire, which if raging unchecked, could in those times quickly cause disaster by destroying the grain which was the chief form of sustenance for man and beast. A few small sidelights on the structures here remain amongst the invaluable Holker deeds.[179] One of 1699 mentions "the Kilnbarn at Barngarth with half the garner next the barn and the beast house under the garner to the third door next the barn,"[180] one of 1724 details "the north granary and stable and beast house under it under the Great Barne".[181] Others detail "the oxenhouse with the Little barn in the barnyard",[182] "a house, two gardens and a barne in the barnyard",[183] "a house croft and hempland there"[184] and "a parcel of land adjoining the Butts in the barnyard",[185] (the latter must almost certainly be in the south part of the area where there was much open space).

Clearly this very extensive collection of structures largely owed their existence to the fact that the priory was a large institution with extensive agricultural needs. If a well-to-do layman had purchased much of the priory property at the Dissolution some part of those structures might have survived. As it was the new lord of the manor at an early stage resided at Holker Hall, so no small part of the priory possessions acquired very minor owners. Inevitably, in the process of time the old agricultural buildings very largely disappeared. The Great Barn was ruinous when in the late 18th century Lord George Cavendish constructed a smallish two-floor building at the top end of the site but this too became ruinous and in 1979 a modern bungalow replaced it.

There is no doubt that most of the land south of the great barn, like the field across the beck which lies between it and the east wall of the main cemetery, was largely used for grazing the cattle whose milk, butter and cheese was one of the main sources of food for the monastery. Significantly, here was a largish building (now totally vanished) which was known as "the dairy". Rather oddly, our knowledge of this structure depends almost entirely on a plan of it shown in a map of the area in a small book published by a Victorian curate of Cartmel, the text of which is almost entirely given over to his sermons.[186] It is difficult not to accept the veracity of the plan he gives which is vigorously delineated and is not a plain rectangle. It seems unlikely to be imaginary, the more so since today cows may still be seen munching placidly in its vicinity.

So far as much of the rest of the Barngarth area is concerned there is no doubt that most of the buildings there – notably the Victorian school, the row of houses on the north side of the Causeway and the very irregular houses at the south end of the road that now runs north and south, are of post-Reformation date. However one building at the southern end until recently showed signs of having housed a small stable with hayloft above, and it is quite feasible that it was part of a small farmyard for the domestic use of the priory. The cows which provided milk for the dairy may well have been housed in this area.

APPENDIX 1: *ACCESS*

ACCESS TO CARTMEL in pre-Reformation days was a very great deal more complex and difficult than it is today, owing to the unusual nature of local geography. Most of the low-lying land between Levens Bridge and Newby Bridge was then virtually uninhabited and impassable. Neither the industry of Barrow-in-Furness nor Lakeland tourism existed to attract the public, whilst almost the only form of transport was the quite expensive horse. Right down to the coming of the railways not much over a century ago, travellers to Furness and Cartmel came mostly from the south and were very few in number, as there was such limited incentives for their journey. For those to whom travel to the area over dry land was regarded as a *sine qua non*, there was necessary a long and circuitous journey, often from Lancaster to Kendal, and thence over Newton to Lancashire-north-of-the-sands. This was an area which was very scantily populated, had nothing that could be ranked as an hotel and next to nothing in the way of inns, whilst the length of the journey was liable to involve the traveller in expenditure of considerable time and money.

Certainly the great mass of visitors to Cartmel and Furness in monastic days came by the curious but much more direct route across the Sands. Lancaster – the principal town for very far around – was the usual starting point. From there most travellers went 3½ miles to the coast at Hest Bank, which became the point of departure northward. There followed a journey of 10 miles over the sands to Kents Bank, whence one old road led over the good dry limestone via Allithwaite to Cartmel, some 3 miles away, and another 3½ miles westward to the little fishing village of Flookburgh. Here the route continued across the channel of the Leven, whose narrow but dangerous waters were somewhat alleviated by a little island which came to take its name from a medieval chapel erected there at an unknown date by a person or persons unknown. The usual landing place in Furness was at Conishead, where there was also a good channel for moorings. Near it was the little monastery of Conishead, founded as a hospital, evidently a little earlier than Cartmel priory. From here over good firm ground a road led to Ulverston, some 21 miles from Lancaster. This lengthy journey was most exacting and by no means free from danger. Safety dictated that it be made around the time of low water, which was not always correctly calculable beforehand, whilst, of course, there were no media of any kind to allow the traveller to check his timing, though the priors of Cartmel and Conishead are each known to have been responsible for ringing bells in time of danger.[187]

In medieval, as in modern times, an unwary traveller might be caught by the tidal bore which sweeps powerfully up the estuary a couple of hours before high water. Fog might suddenly arrive (especially between October and April), the channel might change its course unexpectedly, and unusual weather conditions alter the all-important time of high water. In view of such hazards, hundreds of folk down the ages have had good reason to be grateful to the noble William Marshall, founder of Cartmel priory, who, as we know from official evidence at the time of the Dissolution, successfully instituted and endowed the post of an official who was to guide the public in their crossings; the title accorded to him in the Survey of 1535 being the rather grandiloquent one of "guide and conductor of all the King's people over Sands".[188] At this time he was paid an annual salary of £6 which, with extras, must have made him quite well off by contemporary standards, though his very exacting duties cannot have been widely sought after. A small farm on the road end at Kents Bank was (and still is) a perquisite of his post. The advent of the Reformation in no way diminished the value of the guide's work, so his post was retained. The building of the viaduct, which took the new-fangled railway across the estuary, largely (though not completely) removed the utility of the post, but happily the dwelling and the not very princely salary were retained. Since then the crossing has taken on a new lease of life as a tourist attraction, which has been greatly boosted by television – William Marshall clearly built better than he knew!

For Cartmel priory, geography made transport by sea an essential feature of its economy. Its links with Ireland were useful, whilst local traffic with Lancaster and the priory's fishing right in the estuaries of the Leven and Kent would require at least small craft. Where was the harbour belonging to Cartmel to which we have various references? It is quite certain that nature did not provide here anything remotely comparable to the truly magnificent natural harbour at Peel, whose advantages Furness abbey enjoyed. Most of the coastline here was a slowly shelving one with shallow sandbanks much in evidence. The only place nearby where the very small sea-going craft which the priory possessed could moor, was at the head of a small tidal creek at Grange. The construction of the railway station of Grange, however, has destroyed almost totally any visible proof of its existence. (The name Grange is, of course, significant in itself, for this is the title given to monastic establishments built to store produce and the like.) What may be a sketch of the old grange survived in a sketchbook of about 1800 (now lost). This shows a substantial barn-like structure with a lean-to shed attached but gives no clear indication of its site. The creek along whose banks monastic craft were moored has probably left very slight traces in the small beck and the ornamental pond which it now feeds close to the station. The only oldish documentary mention of this little harbour was found by the industrious Stockdale in the Churchwardens' accounts for 1598, which records the order "12 tonnes of sea coules be bought, being then at Grange."[190]

Cartmel priory's other useful link with the sea was not at Grange, but at Quarry Flat, a place which the railway embankment made totally land bound. As Murray Mitchell has shown, it is quite certain that the local tradition that the stone for building the priory came from here is true, and it is quite likely that it was floated up the Ay at least as far as Cark. Quarry Flat was used as a small harbour at least until the late 18th century, but was totally cut off with the construction of the railway on newly enclosed land. The priory had at Frith Hall a small grange probably used for fishing in the waters of the Leven.

APPENDIX 2: *ROADS*

IT IS QUITE certain that roads were few and very slightly used in the medieval valley of Cartmel, partly because the local terrain was so hostile, but principally because the local population was small and scattered, and lived a life in which trade and commerce played a very small part indeed. The present major road in to South Cumbria via Levens, Lindale and Newton, so heavily worked today, is not yet two centuries old. Before, only a very circuitous route from the south and east to Cartmel and Furness was available, Newby Bridge being virtually unknown.

Locally a brief but firm track led over Hampsfell from the priory's barns at Grange to Cartmel, where at Headless Cross it joined the very old road from Flookburgh via Birkby to Cartmel, anciently known as the Corpse Road since along it came a large proportion of the deceased inhabitants en route to burial at Cartmel. To Headless Cross also came what was in medieval times, little more than a track from Allithwaite. The present Cark road did not exist and that from Holker was little more than a track. What was probably an old but little used route went north over the high ground to Bigland, and that to Newton was also an ancient route, probably more used than most others in the area. Traffic from Newton to Cartmel Fell must have been very minute, and in medieval times Cark was nothing more than a very small hamlet. Odd as it seems today, the only place where old tracks met was the Green whence, as a very post-Reformation signpost still reminds us, travellers could proceed direct to Cartmel, Allithwaite, Flookburgh and Cark. Significantly very near it was the field that formerly housed the gallows of the area.

In medieval days, there is no doubt, the places in the Cartmel area which today are respectable sized villages were all little more than hamlets, with the sole exception of Flookburgh whose one sizeable street had the advantage of being on the main over-sands route which connected Lancaster and the south with Furness. Its position was further strengthened by the fact that its inhabitants in medieval times (and for a long time to come) earned a very respectable living by fishing the well-stocked waters of Morecambe Bay. The place owed its origin to a colony of Viking descent who probably came here from the Isle of Man in the tenth century. Their picturesque Scandinavian dialect is happily still much alive, and in World War II made it possible for a Flookburgh native drafted to Iceland to have no serious language difficulties. But although it evidently acquired the right to hold a market in 1412[191] it found, as did the locals of Cartmel at a later date, that there was not enough commercial activity to allow it to flourish.

APPENDIX 3: *PRIORS OF CARTMEL*

THE VIRTUALLY TOTAL disappearance of the archives of Cartmel Priory and the very inadequate recording of archdeaconry and diocese to which it pertained, makes it impossible to reconstruct more than a very fragmentary list of the priors of the monastery. The following one largely follows that compiled by Professor J. Tait for his article on the priory in the *Victoria County History of Lancs.* (ii. 148).

Daniel	1194/98
William *occ.*	1205, 1208
.Absalon *occ.*	1221, 1230
Simon ? *occ.*	1242
Richard *occ*	1250
John	
William of Walton *occ.*	1279, 1292, 1299
Simon *occ.*	1334
William of Kendal *occ.*	1351, 1354
Richard of Kellett	d. 1380
William Lawrence	1381, ? deprived 1390, 1396
William *occ.*	1441
William Hale *occ.*	1496-8, 1501
Miles Burve *occ.*	1504, 1509
James Grigg *occ.*	1522 *d.* before 1535
Richard Preston *occ.*	1535, surrendered 1536

NOTES & REFERENCES

1 Simeon of Durham, *Hist. de S.Cuth.* (Rolls Series) i 200.

2 *Rot. Cartarum* 216; it has recently been suggested that a chapel may have existed on this very commanding site in Celtic times.

3 W. Farrer, *Lancashire Pipe Rolls* (Liverpool 1902) 311.

4 *Domesday Book of Cheshire* ed: P. Morgan, (Phillimore [Chichester] 1978) 302a and map.

5 S. Painter, *William Marshal, (Baltimore 1933)* is the latest modern study.

6 *L'Histoire de Guillaume le Marechal* ed: P. Meyer (1901).

7 W. Farrer, *Lancs. Pipe Rolls* (1877), 341. Dugdale. *Monasticon Anglicanum* vi. J. C. Dickinson, *The origins of the Austin canons and their introduction into England* (1950), 292. VCH Lancs. ii 143-8.

8 W. Farrer, *Lancashire Pipe Rolls* (1897) *pp.* 341. As Dr Farrer pointed out in 1897, the 17th century assertion that the priory was founded in 1188, is patently untrue. Unhappily Church Council disregarded this fact (of which I firmly informed them) and insisted on celebrating the Octo-Centenary in 1988. Recent study has shown that the foundation charter was drawn up between late 1189 and March 1196 (D. Crouch *William Marshall* 1990).

9 D. Knowles and C. N. L. Brooke, *The heads of religious houses in England and Wales 940-1216* (CUP) 158.

10 Seynt Austyn order, of the first fundation of Willylm Marshall, the yeerle of Pembroke in the year of our Lord anno mcii and before his death xvj year, ye iij[c] anno regis Johannis. B.M. MS Harl. 604 f.123 (106).

11 *Cal. Pap. Lett.* iv 366.

12 *The Lonsdale Magazine* ed. J. Briggs, (Kirkby Lonsdale iii 1821) 89.

13 Unpublished information.

14 *The Furness Coucher Book* ed. J. Brownbill (Chetham Soc.) ii pt, ii, 88-90.

15 J. Stockdale, *Annals of Cartmel* (Ulverston 1872), 17=Lancs. Rec. Sec. i 29.

16 *Rot. Cartarum* 216.

17 *VCH Lancs* ii 268.

18 *ibid.* 273n, 278n, 280.

19 *ibid.* 278n; the canons had earlier acquired "Madonscales" in Broughton.

20 *ibid.* 277n.

21 *ibid.* 257 – this may have been held at Flookburgh.

22 *Rot. Cart.* 216.

23 *ibid.* 8.

24 Baines, *Hist. of Lancs.* ii (1870) 677.

25 *VCH Lancs.* viii 138.

26 *ibid.* 135-6.

27 *ibid.* 249-50.

28 *ibid.* 41n. 131.

29 *ibid.* 277.

30 *ibid.* 273.

31 *ibid.* 272.

32 *ibid.* 274 n.8.

33 *ibid.* 277.

34 below

35 *VCH Lancs.* viii 277.

36 *Lancs. and Cheshire deeds in the Public Record Office* ed. W. D. Selby (1882) 89-91.

37 *Final concords of the county of Lancaster* ed. W. Farrer, (1899),

39-40.

38 *ibid.*

39 *Records of Kendale* ed. W. Farrer ii (1924) 214-6.

40 *ibid.* 8 – the priory owned a ferry here.

41 *Taxatio Ecclesiastica 1291* (Rec. Com), 308.

42 *VCH Lancs.* viii 276 quoting D. Lancs. Rentals and Surveys, bdle. 4 no. 12.

43 The chapel adjoined the route over Sands from Lancaster to Furness which was easily the principal way there in medieval times.

44 *VCH Lancs.* viii 276.

45 *ibid.*

46 *ibid.*

47 G. A. Behrens, "Conservation work on the Cartmel Fell figure of Christ." CWAS lxxxii (1982) 125-34.

48 *VCH Lancs.* viii 262.

49 W. Farrer, *Records of Kendale*, ii 192.

50 *VCH Lancs.* viii 181 n. 20 – the place was perhaps founded for folk making the dangerous crossing of the sands to Cartmel.

51 *ibid.* viii 249-50.

52 Baines, *Hist of Lancs.* ii 677-8.

53 A. Gwynn and R. N. Hadcock, *Medieval religious houses of Ireland* (1980) *passim.*

54 Dugdale *Mon.* vi 455.

55 *VCH Lancs.* ii 144.

56 *Register of St. Thomas Dublin* (Rolls Series) 357-8.

57 *Cal. Doc. Ireland,* nos. 491, 1861, 1867.

58 *Cal. Close Rolls* 21 Hen. III p. 401. Similar licences followed – ibid. 1232-47, 241, 127, 1272-81 896; in 1316 – ibid. 1313-7, 549.

59 *Cal. Pat. R. 1321-4,* 107.

60 *ibid.* 1281-92 468, 509, 510.

61 *ibid.* 1292-1301 483.

62 *ibid.* 1307-13 280.

63 *ibid.* 1307-13 509.

64 *ibid.* 1307-13 90.

65 *ibid.* 1313-17 211.

66 *ibid.* 1313-17 611.

67 *ibid.* 1317-21 402.

68 *ibid.* 1345-48 348.

69 *ibid.* 1350-54 383.

70 *ibid.* 1354-58 275.

71 *ibid.* 1354-58 567.

72 *ibid.* 1361-64 257.

73 *ibid.* 1381-85 62.

74 *ibid.* 1381-8.

75 *ibid.* 1391-96 196.

76 *Crede Mihi* ed. J. T. Gilbert (Dublin 1897) 97-100.

77 *ibid.*

78 *ibid.* Cal. Pat. R.

79 P.R.O. SC II/935 m.5.

80 Bains, *Hist of Lancs.* ii 678.

81 *Lancs. Final Concords* (Chetham Soc.) i 111.

82 *Register of Walter Grey,* (Surtees Soc. Vol. 56 1870) 31.

83 *Cal. Pap. Lett.* iii 557.

84 *Cal. Pap. Lett.* IV 366.

85 *Reg. Wickwane* (Surt. Soc.) 148-50.

86 *Reg. le Romeyn* (Surt. Soc.) 337, 350-1.

87 *Cal. Pap. Lett.* III 557.

88 *ibid.* V 32.

89 H. E. Salter, *Chapters of the Augustinian Canons,* (Oxford 1922) 2-3.

90 *ibid.* 37.

91 *ibid.* 42.

92 *ibid.* 80.

93 *Cal. Pap. Lett.* IV 371.

94 *ibid.* V 32.

95 J. C. Dickinson "Three pre-Reformation documents concerning South Cumbria" Cumb. West. Arch. Soc. Trans. NS lxxxvi (1936) p. 130.

96 Knowles and Hadcock *op. cit,* 153

97 below p.

98 *Chronicon de Lanercost* (Maitland Club) 233.

99 *ibid.*

100 *Taxatio* 309.

101 *ibid.* 328.

102 *Rotuli Parliamentorum* VI 397.

103 *Cal. Let. Pat.* 1485-94, 135.

104 see below.

105 *Registers of the Archdeaconry of Richmond 1361-77* ed. A. Hamilton Thompson (*Yorks. Arch. Journal*) XXV 200.

106 *ibid.* 215-6.

107 *ibid.* xxxii (1935) 116.

108 above.

109 Corpus Christ College, Cambridge MS 170 ff. 144, 123.

110 D. of Lancs. Surveys pf10. 4 no. 12.

111 Salter, *op. cit.* 140.

112 below.

113 PRO Exchequer, T. R. Misc. Bks. no. 149 (14 Hen. VIII) p. 26.

114 W. de Gray Birch, *Catalogue of Seals in the British Museum*, nos. 2882, 2883.

115 W. Dugdale, *Monasticon Anglicanum* vi 454.

116 C. Haigh, Reformation and Resistance in Tudor Lancashire (C.U.P. 1975).

117 *ibid.*

118 *ibid.*

119 *ibid.* 120.

120 *ibid.* 126.

121 *ibid.*

122 *ibid.*

123 *ibid.*

124 *VCH Lancs.* viii 263-4.

125 *ibid.* 262 n. 75.

126 *ibid.* 257, 275.

127 *ibid.* 137 n. 6.

128 *ibid.*

129 *VCH Lancs.* ii 148.

130 Stockdale *op. cit.* 47-8.

131 *ibid.* 49

132 *VCH Lancs.* viii 263 n. 82.

133 *The Holker Muniments* ed. R. Sharpe France (Penrith 1950) p. 27.

134 *VCH Lancs.* viii 263.

135 *ibid.*

136 *VCH Lancs.* viii 254-85 *passim.*

137 J. L. Petit "Cartmel Priory Church, Lancashire" *Arch.* Journ. xxvii (1870) 81-91 – a very illuminating essay.

138 *Stockdale* 108.

139 below.

140 *Stockdale* 47.

141 *ibid.* 108.

142 *ibid.* 47.

143 *ibid.* 50.

144 *ibid.* 81.

145 *ibid.* 47.

146 *ibid.* 50.

147 *ibid.* 53.

148 *ibid.* 108.

149 J. C. Dickinson in *CWAS – NS* LXXXVI (1986) 129-30.

150 *ibid.* 151.

152 Stockdale. 142.

153 *HMCR Westmorland* 1936), 46.

154 *ibid.* 47.

155 J. Blair, unpublished.

156 G. L. Remnant, *Catalogue of Misericords* 1969, p. 78. Suggests a rather earlier date – and considers that the Cartmel seats may have links with those at Carlisle.

157 *Stockdale* 75.

158 E. E. Sharpe, *Decorated Windows – a series of illustrations* (1840) nos. 22, 23.

159 J. C. Dickinson, "The Harrington Tomb at Cartmel priory church" CWAS New Series LXXXV (1985) 115-22.

160 *Stockdale* 546.

161 These have recently been returned to the church.

162 CWAS (New Series) XXV 373-4.

163 *The Antiquaries Journal* XXIII (1943) 28.

164 Crossley, *English Church Monuments* (1933) 67.
165 This gift is recorded on his memorial now on the north wall of the nave.
166 *Stockdale* 110.
167 W. R. M. Chaplin *The Bells of the priory church of Cartmel* (1937) (pamphlet).
168 *Stockdale* 53.
169 *ibid.* 57.
170 Oxford, Bodl. Lib.
171 *Stockdale* 53-6.
172 Lancashire Record Office DDN/4/3.
173 *ibid.*
174 *The Holker Muniments*, R. Sharpe France (Penrith 1950), p. 8.
175 Oxford Bodl. Lib.
176 *The Holker Muniments*, 27-8.
177 *VCH Lancs.* viii 259 n. 64.
178 *The Holker Muniments*, 27.
179 It is most unfortunate that none of the pre-Reformation deeds concerning this area have survived.
180 *ibid.* 10.
181 *ibid.* p. 10.
182 *ibid.* p. 28.
183 *ibid.* p. 9.
184 *ibid.* p. 28.
185 *ibid.* p. 9.
186 W. ffoliot, *Cartmel parish and parish church*, (London 1854).
187 Haigh, *op. cit.*
188 *Valer Ecclesiasticus*, V 272.
189 A. M. Wakefield, *Cartmel Priory and Sketches of North Lonsdale.* (Grange over Sands 1909) – opposite p. 49: The illustration is here given the title "The first school in Grange" and recorded as "From a pencil sketch in an old Sketch Book". It is highly unlikely that there was a school at Grange until a very late date. The building depicted has a large and massive central portion apparently of three floors doubtless originally used largely for storage, and having a small lean-to section on one side and what was probably a sizeable barn on the other with the usual capacious entrance.
190 *Stockdale* 38-9.
191 VCH Lancs. VIII 275 4257.

Index